RUDOLF STEINER (1861–1925) called his spiritual philosophy 'anthroposophy', meaning 'wisdom of the human being'. As a highly developed seer, he based his work on direct knowledge and perception of spiritual dimensions. He initiated a modern and universal 'science of spirit', accessible to anyone willing to exercise clear and unprejudiced thinking.

From his spiritual investigations Steiner provided suggestions for the renewal of many activities, including education (both general and special), agriculture, medicine, economics, architecture, science, philosophy, religion and the arts. Today there are thousands of schools, clinics, farms and other organizations involved in practical work based on his principles. His many published works feature his research into the spiritual nature of the human being, the evolution of the world and humanity, and methods of personal development. Steiner wrote some 30 books and delivered over 6000 lectures across Europe. In 1924 he founded the General Anthroposophical Society, which today has branches throughout the world.

Victorious spirit
flame through the faintness
of hesitant souls.
Burn up ego's self-craving,
ignite compassion,
so that selflessness,
the life-stream of mankind
wells up as the source
of spirit's rebirth.

MICHAELMAS

Festivals

Also available:

RUDOLF STEINER

MICHAELMAS
An Introductory Reader

Compiled with an introduction,
commentary and notes by
Matthew Barton

Sophia Books

Sophia Books
An imprint of Rudolf Steiner Press
Hillside House, The Square
Forest Row, RH18 5ES

www.rudolfsteinerpress.com

Published by Rudolf Steiner Press 2007

For earlier English publications of individual selections please
see pp. 143–4

The material by Rudolf Steiner was originally published in
German in various volumes of the 'GA' (*Rudolf Steiner
Gesamtausgabe* or Collected Works) by Rudolf Steiner Verlag,
Dornach. This authorized volume is published by permission of
the Rudolf Steiner Nachlassverwaltung, Dornach (for further
information see pp. 147–8)

All translations revised by Matthew Barton

*The editor would like to thank Margaret Jonas, librarian at Rudolf
Steiner House, for her invaluable help in locating volumes used in
compiling this book.*

This selection and translation © Rudolf Steiner Press 2007

All rights reserved. No part of this publication may be
reproduced, stored in a retrieval system, or transmitted, in any
form or by any means, electronic, mechanical, photocopying
or otherwise, without the prior permission of the publishers

A catalogue record for this book is available from the British
Library

ISBN 978 185584 159 8

Cover by Andrew Morgan
Typeset by DP Photosetting, Neath, West Glamorgan
Printed by Cromwell Press Ltd., Trowbridge, Wiltshire

Contents

Introduction

Michaelmas Day, or the festival of St Michael and All Angels (29 September), does not even figure on the calendar on my wall. In traditional farming communities there was a large number of country customs at Michaelmas (including stealing your neighbour's horse with impunity!), but nowadays little is associated with it apart from the name of a university term, a day when quarter rents are due or the day for choosing magistrates. Perhaps the latter, at least, contains the faint trace of a lost insight into a dimension of being — and indeed an actual being — which Rudolf Steiner focuses on in the lecture extracts compiled here. What is a magistrate after all? Derived from the Latin *magister* or master, it is clearly connected with authority — something, however, which we cannot properly exercise without a degree of *self*-mastery. A magistrate enforces the law but must also weigh up the merits of each case by using his or her own power of judgement and intuition; and the Michaelic qualities Steiner returns to on several occasions include a conscious quality of inner judgement, resolve and decisive action, informed by the forces of the heart. *Chambers Dictionary* also tells me that 'magistery' is a term in alchemy referring to a 'transmuting agent, a precipitate or any sovereign remedy'. In these lectures Steiner speaks often of the need for a transformation of the human mind and heart; and in a couple of passages, indeed, he mentions that the time of autumn, when natural forces are waning, can be understood as a season when the human spirit separates from the natural world and comes to a sense of its own, independent existence, much as a substance in solution separates out, forming a precipitate and leaving a purified fluid behind.

The year is a cycle which we can accompany with our feeling and awareness: a sequence of changing phenomena in the external world but also a greater image of processes at work in the human being. At one time (during spring and summer) we are intimately linked to all its flourishing physical processes as an image of our own physical life; at another (autumn and winter), we separate from its waning and death just as the spirit can separate from its 'suspension' in the body, becoming more conscious of its non-physical existence. The festival of Michaelmas which Steiner wished to reinstate and wholly reinvigorate is one which he believed was particularly vital in our time: the celebration of a new age which had dawned, when human beings

can go beyond the constraints of a narrow materialism and at the same time find their way to true
fellowship with one another. He believed a
Michaelmas festival worthy of the name would do
more to address the social ills of our time than any
amount of abstract debate and well-meaning but
impotent measures. Typically, he does not dictate
what form such a festival would take but — a
Michael quality — leaves us completely free, simply
urging us to create the right conditions in ourselves
out of which such a festival could authentically
develop.

The picture of St Michael vanquishing the
dragon, various versions of which readers may
know from art history or legend, is one which
Steiner conjures again before us as an image — in
fact a reality — of a battle waged continually
between different forces within us: those which
harness us to a spellbound enchantment in the
material world, and those which we ourselves must
activate to penetrate a veil of illusion, to truly meet
nature, ourselves, each other and greater realities.
This is also something, as Steiner emphasizes,
which requires courage — a quality he connects
particularly with the beginning of autumn.

As trees grow bare of leaves, revealing, as it were,
the skeleton of things, it is easy to sense layers of
physical protection falling away from us as greater,

lonelier spaces open up. This season, at the fine transition between natural life and death, but equally between a sleepier nature consciousness and a waking consciousness of self, feels like that sword blade in fairy tales that is laid as a sharp reminder between two who are not married — between, you could say, nature and spirit, which divide from each other at this time of year.

But not just at this time of year. Steiner stresses that, since we are not merely natural beings, we can have all seasons in us simultaneously. He continually returns to the theme of our modern era, finding a particular correspondence between the start of autumn and our present state and stage of evolution. We are no longer sustained by past certainties and by a mothering natural world. We have risen above it, coming far adrift in the process from a harmonious balance with ourselves and our environment — a loss so beautifully lamented in Chief Seattle's address to the conquering white man.[1] This evolutionary transition — as people the world over are increasingly aware — is forcing us to awaken to the consequences of our own actions in many different spheres, asking us to exercise moral judgement and take responsibility for ourselves and the planet. To reconnect consciously. And increasingly it is becoming clear, in a way similar to the wider vistas that open up as leaves fall, that a battle is raging between these developing forces of sensitivity, awareness and responsibility and those of — really there is no other word — demonic self-interest, social divisiveness and materialism, often, let's not deceive ourselves, combined within each one of us. So the battle is with and within ourselves.

Just two aspects of our age are enough, perhaps, to highlight the nature of this battle. I'd like to accentuate each and give an accompanying image that occurred to me in relation to them. Our era, of course, promotes a widespread worship and culture of youth, a pervasive trait that can easily make people feel that the elderly have no value, that the flourish and beauty of youth is the only worthy human state. This is not just the worship of youth and beauty, though, but the adulation of all things physical, the denial of soul and spiritual qualities which, as Steiner points out, can only shine through — like autumn colours — as physical attributes wane. Of course this depends on *how* we age: whether we cling desperately to physical life, lamenting each wrinkle, or allow non-physical qualities to rise up in us, revealing our true, non-physical nature like the sun shining through thinning clouds. Recently I was walking in the grounds of a National Trust estate and I saw a wonderful sight, a lively young girl and a bent old man together. I do not know if he was her father or grandfather, but there was something blessed about the atmosphere between them, she leaping to touch a branch, he hobbling slowly but with a genuinely illumined, unhurried air. Somehow one could sense the girl's deep, unspoken love of the old man, and his of her; and this struck me as a powerful image of the relationship between the physical and the spiritual, how each age can honour the other, and how the summer of youth can give way gracefully and willingly to the autumn of age and its spiritual gifts.

The other image is that of the archangel Michael as the countenance of Christ. Steiner mentions this several times. Our age is one in which the head often predominates. So many of us spend a great deal of time no longer gazing out into the world but into the interior of the computer's artificial 'head', into a virtual reality that detaches us from the world and each other while artificially 'connecting' us — and increasingly straitjackets and mechanizes our thinking. Steiner describes the face of Michael, in contrast, as outward gazing, silent but expectant, waiting for our courageous and conscious deeds. Michael, says Steiner, is a being who does not aspire to the pride of the separate human intellect, but who reflects cosmic intelligence such as we find at work throughout the natural world.

The other day, in early October, I went out into my

garden in the slanting morning sunshine and found a spider busily weaving its web. Spiders get a bad press, but I was transfixed by the light illuminating the filaments of the developing web, the radiating spokes like a small sun, and the extraordinary intelligence active in the spider as it deftly worked its way round and inwards from the web's outer edge, hitching each small section of thread — spun from itself — to the web's shining surface. You may say that this was all in aid of Darwinian survival, to entrap other creatures. While true on one level, at another the web also seemed like a transparent window or face through which cosmic law was working, an utterance from the heart of nature to the human heart. The intelligence in nature is innocent, unconscious and intuitive — a stage we cannot go back to. We are a long way from becoming such clear, but now conscious, vessels for the cosmos to work through — but perhaps it is time to make a start.

Except for the final lecture in this volume, which is given in its entirety, the passages collected here range from single paragraphs to long extracts. Steiner developed his lectures into an art form in the best sense, and the reader is referred to the original, complete lectures for the 'total experience' and context from which these passages are drawn.

Matthew Barton

SINKING EARTH, RISING SPIRIT

1. Reading More Deeply

Extract from a lecture given in Vienna on
1 October 1923

*Read in a different way, says Steiner, if what you read is
going to transform you and come to life within you. This
heartfelt reading and engagement can also be applied to
nature itself, which Steiner urges us to experience deeply
and inwardly, feeling both our profound connection to
and necessary separation from it. This deep reading, he
says, will counter the impotence of abstract ideas that are
incapable of effecting real change, and could feed into a
Michaelmas festival imbued with real, transformative
power.*

If you read a book or a lecture cycle on anthroposophy just as you read any other book — that is, in
the same abstract way — there is no point in reading
anthroposophical[2] literature at all. In that case I
would advise you to read cookery books or tech-
nical books on mechanics: that would be more
useful. Or read about 'How to become a Good
Businessman'. Reading books or listening to lec-

tures on anthroposophy has sense only when you realize that to receive its messages a totally different frame of mind is called for from the one involved in the gleaning of other information. This is confirmed by the fact that those who nowadays consider themselves to be very intelligent regard anthroposophic literature as mad ...

And indeed, the conclusions reached by anthroposophy are very different from what emanates from other quarters. And I must say that a certain policy adhered to by some of our friends, that of making anthroposophy generally palatable by talking down the discrepancies between it and the superficial views of others, is not one I can approve of at all ... What is needed is a totally different orientation and attitude of soul if the message of anthroposophy is to be considered plausible, comprehensible, intelligent—instead of mad.

But given this different orientation, not only the human intellect but also the human heart and soul will soon undergo a schooling that renders it more sensitive to impressions. It will no longer feel winter merely as the time for donning a heavy coat, or summer as the signal for shedding various articles of clothing; but rather it will learn to feel the subtle transitions occurring in the course of the year, from the cold snows of winter to sultry midsummer. We shall learn to sense the course of the year as we do the expressions of a living, soul-endowed being. Indeed, the proper study of anthroposophy can bring us to the point at which we feel the manifestations of the seasons as we do the assent or dissent in the soul of a friend. Just as in the words of a friend and in the whole attitude of his soul we can perceive the warm heartbeat of a soul-endowed being whose manner of speaking to us is quite different from that of a lifeless thing, so nature, hitherto mute, will begin to speak to us as though from her soul. In the cycle of the seasons we will learn to feel evolving soul. We will learn to listen to what the year as a great living being has to tell us, instead of occupying ourselves only with smaller living beings. We will then find our place in the whole, soul-endowed cosmos.

But then, when summer passes into autumn and winter approaches, something very special will speak to us out of nature. Someone who has gradually acquired the sensitive feeling for nature just described — and anthroposophists will notice in due time that this can indeed be developed in the soul through anthroposophical practice — will learn to distinguish between nature consciousness, engendered during spring and summer, and self-awareness which thrives in the autumn and winter. What is nature consciousness? When spring comes the earth unfolds its sprouting, blossoming life.

And if I react to this in the right way, if I let all that spring really encompasses speak within me — although I do not have to be aware of it since it speaks in the unconscious depths as well — if I achieve this then I do not merely say that flowers are blooming and plants germinating, but I also feel a true concord with nature, and can say: My higher ego blooms in the flower, germinates in the plant. Nature consciousness is engendered only by learning to participate in all that develops in nature's burgeoning and unfolding life. To be able to germinate with the plant, to bear fruit with the plant, means to pass beyond one's own inner self and become one with nature. The concept of developing spirituality does not mean becoming abstract, but means following the spirit in its developing and unfolding being. And if by participating in the germinating, the flowering and the bearing of fruit we develop this delicate feeling for nature during the spring and summer, we prepare ourselves to live in devotion to the universe, to the firmament, precisely at the height of summer. Then every tiny glow-worm will be a revelation to us of the cosmos. Every breeze at midsummer will proclaim to us the cosmic principle alive within earthly things.

But then — if we have learned to feel with nature, to blossom with the flowers, to germinate with the seeds, to take part in fruiting—then, because we have learned to dwell in nature with our own being, we cannot help inwardly experiencing autumn and winter too. He who has learned to live with nature in the spring learns also to die with nature in the autumn ...

But we must not die, nor let ourselves be over-powered. We can live united with burgeoning, blossoming nature, and in so doing we can develop our nature consciousness. But when we experience the dying in nature, this is a challenge to us to oppose this death with the creative forces of our own inner being. Then the spirit and soul, our true self-awareness, will come to life within us. And by sharing in nature's dying during the autumn and winter, we will, to the highest degree, awaken our own self-awareness. In this way we evolve as human beings. We transform ourselves in the course of the seasons by experiencing this alter-nation of nature consciousness and self-awareness. When we participate in nature's dying that is the time when our inner life force must awaken ...

It is vital that anthroposophical knowledge should stream into the human heart and soul as a real force. This will lead us from today's dry, abstract, though precise concepts to a living, heartfelt engagement with life, which can engender something as full of life as was in olden times the glorious image of Michael in battle with the dragon ... Only the living spirit, which speaks to us in nature in the same way as the human soul speaks to us, can enter our hearts and minds in a vitalizing and uplifting way. When this does occur, our hearts will derive power from the enlightenment transformed within them, and these are the very powers we need in society. During the last three or four centuries mankind has simply acquired the habit of considering all nature, and human existence as well, in intellectual, abstract concepts. And now that humanity is faced with the great problems of social chaos, people try to solve these too with the same intellectual means. But this will never lead to anything but chimeras. A fully developed human heart is essential for addressing social issues. But no one can possess this without also finding his relationship to the whole cosmos, and in particular its spiritual attributes.

When the human heart and soul has received spiritual awareness into itself, engendered by the transformation from nature consciousness (spring and summer) to self-awareness (autumn and winter) then the social problems of today will start to be resolved ...

We must dwell on all this if we are to consider adding the autumn festival, the Michael festival to the festivals of Christmas, Easter and St John—

which have become mere shadows. How wonderful it would be if this Michael festival could be celebrated at the end of September with the whole power of the human heart! But never must it be celebrated simply by making certain external arrangements that engender nothing but abstract impressions. A Michael festival calls for human beings who feel in their souls in fullest measure everything that can activate spiritual awareness . . .

2. The Human Earthworm

Extract from a lecture given in Vienna on
30 September 1923

*We should lift our gaze, says Steiner, rather than staying
down in the comfortable dark ...*

And what is the human being really as far as his
awareness is concerned? Well, he is really an
earthworm — and worse: an earthworm for whom it
never rains! In certain localities where there is a
great deal of rain it is so pleasant to see the worms
coming out of the ground — we must take care not to
tread on them ... and then we reflect: those poor
little chaps are down there underground all the
time and only surface when it rains; but if it does
not rain they have to stay below. Now the materialist of today is just such an earthworm — but one
for whom it never rains. For, if we continue with the
simile, the rain would be spiritual enlightenment
pouring into us, for otherwise we would always be
crawling about down there where there is no light.
Today humanity must overcome this earthworm

nature: it must emerge, must surface into the light, the spiritual light of day. And the call for a Michael festival is the call for the spiritual light of day.

3. Spirit Shines Brighter as Physical Matter Fades

Extract from a lecture given in Dornach on
2 April 1923

Our spiritual life depends on declining physical life. As scientists know, the brain is the least living part of us and our thoughts depend on the death of cells.

It is true that spring is fair, and it is a fine capacity of the human soul to perceive the beauty of spring, the growing, sprouting, burgeoning life. But to be able to perceive also when the leaves fade and take on their autumn colouring, when the animals creep away to hibernate, to be able to feel how in the sensible, which is dying away, the gleaming, shining, soul-spiritual element arises — to be able to perceive how, with the yellowing of the leaves comes a decline and fading of burgeoning life, but how the sensible fades and becomes yellow so that the spiritual can live in the yellowing; to be able to perceive how in the falling of leaves the ascent of the spirit takes place, how the spiritual is a counterpart to the fading sense world: this would ensoul the human being in autumn as a perceptive feeling for the spirit. Then we would prepare ourselves in the right way for the time of Christmas.

Anthroposophical science of the spirit should permeate us with the truth that our spiritual life depends on declining physical life. Whenever we think, the physical matter in our nerves is destroyed; thought struggles its way forth from perishing matter. To feel a thought arising in oneself—an idea gleaming up in the human soul, the whole human organism—as akin to the yellowing leaves, withering foliage, the shrivelling and fading of the plant world in nature, to feel the kinship of our spiritual essence with nature's decline can give us the impulse that strengthens our will and points us to the permeation of our will with spirituality.

MICHAEL AND THE DRAGON

4. Swelling Desire, Clarifying Consciousness

Extract from a lecture given in Stuttgart on
15 October 1923

In this passage Steiner emphasizes the correlation between processes at work in the wide cosmos and those within human beings. He relates what he calls the 'sulphurous' processes of animal desires in us to similar processes which expand out into the cosmos at midsummer. The counter-force to such animal desire is the iron at work both within our blood and in the form of meteoric iron in the cosmos. In describing these close interconnections between the human being and the cosmos, Steiner conjures the ancient image of Michael and the dragon as the embodiment of these warring forces, urging us to picture this vividly as a reality that directly affects us. As always, Steiner is trying to make us see vividly in living pictures and imaginations rather than cold abstractions — in terms of real beings rather than mere 'forces'.

In all that the earth reveals, in stone and plant, in all creatures, spiritual beings live — not merely a general, vague spirituality, but separate spirit beings, nature spirits.[3] These nature spirits enclose themselves during the winter in the bowels of the earth; they are breathed in, as it were, by the earth and dwell there. When spring comes the earth breathes out, as it were, her spirituality and then these nature spirits strive upwards. They aspire upwards with the forces of springing, sprouting life; they are active in the life which is felt in the radiant light and sun-warmed air, streaming upwards within it. And as we approach St John's Day[4] and the time of midsummer, then in the heights above us, if we look up to them, a picture is revealed to us, embodied in the forms of the clouds, embodied powerfully too in lightning and thunder, embodied in all the elements of the weather above us, of all that lived during winter as nature spirits deep in the dark bosom of the earth. During winter we must look down to the earth and feel, or behold, how hidden beneath the covering of snow nature spirits are working, so that out of winter spring will come again, and summer on the productive earth.

But if in summer we look down to the earth then it seems impoverished by the loss of those nature spirits. They have gone out into the wide universe, uniting themselves with cloud formations and everything that human sight encounters in the heights above. In all the ways I have mentioned

they have streamed up to the heights, taking with
them, in extremely rarefied form, a highly rarefied
dilution, what manifests outwardly as crude and
lifeless sulphur. And in fact these nature spirits, as
they billow and surge in cloud forms and suchlike
during the height of summer, weave and live pre-
eminently in the sulphur that is present there in
extraordinarily subtle form. If we could speed
through these high reaches of our earthly world
during the height of summer with a sort of tasting-
feeling sense, we would be aware of a sulphurous
taste and even smell, though of a very dilute,
rarefied and subtle kind. What develops up there,
however, under the influence of the sun's warmth
and light is akin to the process that goes on in the
human organism when cravings, wishes, emotions
and so on come welling up. Those who have a
faculty for beholding and feeling such things know
that the nature spirits in the heights at midsummer
live in an element which is as much saturated with
desire as is the desire life bound up with the human
being's animal nature—the animal part of us in
which we too are 'sulphurized' or permeated with
sulphur in highly dilute form. At midsummer we
see as it were our lower aspect, all that is animal
desire in us, arching in natural formation above us,
filled with the life of nature spirits. What we thus
recognize in its sulphurous quality when it lives

and weaves in human nature can be called the ahrimanic.[5] The ahrimanic actually lives in this element. So we can also say that when, in high summer time, we turn spiritual vision towards the heights, then the ahrimanic is revealed to us in sulphurous desires permeating the cosmos. So if we think of our close connection with this whole cosmic process, we have to say: The earth absorbs in winter what exists in us as our lower nature and spreads over it crystalline snow, and by so doing the earth receives the ahrimanic into itself. And in high summer, when the ahrimanic is free, it works as cosmic desires out in the wide reaches of the air...

And now we see how this ahrimanic desire element, this animal desire nature in us turned inside out into the cosmos, as it were, is opposed by another force. The cosmos provides a counter-force to the force that brings the human being into subjection through his emotions, dragging him down below the human to the animal level, a force externalized at midsummer high above us. This counter-force is visible in those remarkable phenomena which fall to earth from time to time as products of the cosmos, and contain meteoric iron. If you examine a piece of meteoric iron you have before you a remarkable testimony to the iron dispersed throughout the cosmos. The shooting stars which come so frequently in August reveal this counter-force of nature opposing the desire element present there in the heights at this time. This cosmic iron condensed to meteoric stones is, you can say, the arrows which the cosmos shoots into the animal desire element manifest there.

So we can look with understanding and awe upon the wisdom of the cosmos. We know of course that human beings need this animal desire precisely because they can only develop the forces that make them fully human by first overcoming it. And we could not have this desire nature, this animalizing element, if the same animal desire element were not a part of the cosmos also. The sulphur then, the sulphurous, ahrimanic element is, as it were, one pole of the cosmos; and the arrows discharged by the cosmos to combat this sulphurous element are concentrated in meteoric iron—the meteoric projectiles, you can say, of the universe.

Now the human being is a true microcosm, really a little cosmos. Everything that manifests in the great world outside in gigantic and majestic phenomena such as meteors also manifests within us, in the inward nature of what we are ourselves as physical beings. For the physical being is only an expression, a manifestation of our spiritual being. And so in a certain way we bear within ourselves, emanating from our lower animal nature, the sulphurous element. We must say that this sulphurous, ahrimanic element storms through the human organism, stirring up our desires and emotions. We feel it within us. We behold it at high summer outside us, in the cosmic mist of desire above our heads. But we also behold how into this over-arching cosmic mist shoot the iron arrows of shooting stars, of meteoric phenomena, cleansing and clarifying it, acting as an opposite pole to animal desires. For through this shooting in of meteoric iron arrows from the cosmos, the mist above us, the animal desire of high summer, is purified.

And what takes place in majesty and grandeur out there in the cosmos goes on continually in us too. We produce tiny iron particles in our blood, in combination with other substances. And while on the one hand there pulses through our blood the sulphurizing process, it is countered by the other pole, the iron inside us, bringing about the same process as meteoric iron causes in the wider cosmos. In our relationship to the cosmos, therefore, we can picture the flashing, scintillating meteoric element we find there as the counterpart of what, within us, is a million upon million-fold sparking from the iron in our blood. This frees us, cleansing and clarifying us from the sulphurizing process which is also active in the blood itself.

Thus we are inwardly a reflection of the cosmos.

In the cosmos this process is accomplished during the height of summer. Because we are to some extent emancipated from natural cycles, we continually have midsummer within us, together with all the other seasons, just as our past experiences also remain with us through memory. Outwardly they have passed away, but inwardly they remain. In the same way we retain the macrocosm within us, as microcosm. What we carry in our physical body, however, we must grasp in soul and spirit, must grow able to experience in ourselves. We must learn to experience this meteoric shooting of the blood iron into the blood sulphur as freedom, or initiative, as the strength of our will. Otherwise it remains at best an animal or vegetative process in us. We become fully human in soul and spirit when we consciously grasp the processes at work in us, such as this iron-sulphur process, send the soul and spirit into them as an impulse. It is similar to making a tool or instrument, and knowing how to handle it properly — then we can use it. In the same way, when we know how to handle it, we can make use, through our will, of this iron and sulphur process that works and lives in us.

*   *   *

When we feel all this in full earnestness, then a cosmic imagination forms in us ... not one deriving from fantasy but the true expression of a process permeating the world and the human being — in this case a process embedded in the cycle of the seasons.

The imagination or picture which comes to us through this experience is one that springs from inwardly accompanying the year's course from midsummer on towards the end of summer, the beginning of autumn. From this experience the living figure of Michael arises. From the experience I described, the figure of Michael is revealed in his fight with the dragon, with our animal nature, the sulphurizing process. When one understands what is actually going on in these phenomena then the soul, which takes its own form and origin from the interweaving life forces of the cosmos, simply engenders the fight of Michael with the dragon. Michael himself appears as the outward expression of what is working out in the cosmos in the battle with animalized desires. But he appears with a sword pointing towards man's higher nature; and we picture Michael rightly when we see his pointing sword as the cosmically smelted and forged iron. Out of spiritual cloud formations, you can say, the figure of Michael appears to us with positive, searching and directing gaze, his eyes like a guiding sign, his gaze sent outwards, never drawn back into himself; and the arm of Michael appears to us in the midst of a sparkling shower of meteoric iron, as though this were molten in forces of cosmic desire and fused together again to form Michael's flaming sword.

We picture Michael rightly when we think of his countenance as woven from the golden light of summer, with a positive gaze directing us outwards, like a ray of light from within sent actively out. We picture Michael rightly when we see his outstretched arm flaming with flashing sprays of meteor iron that fuse together into the sword with which he shows humanity the way from animal nature to higher human nature; with which he points the way from the summer season, when we are most at one with nature, are most imbued with nature consciousness, to that other season of autumn, when we can only continue to live united with nature if we share in her dying, the death into which she plunges. But it would be terrible for the human being only to share with nature, as autumn comes, this natural path of death, this self-destruction. When we experience spring we yield ourselves, if we are wholly human, to nature in her sprouting, waxing, flourishing. If we are full human beings we blossom with each blossom, sprout with every leaf, for then her will is to live, and we share this impulse of life with her. We do well to immerse ourselves in nature at this season. But in autumn we cannot unfold this nature consciousness in ourselves, for doing so would mean sharing in the experience of paralysis and death she undergoes. We should not accompany her in that direction, but instead increase our self-reliant strength. Just as we must experience living nature in our own life forces, so must we set against dying nature, against death, the human self. Nature consciousness must be transformed into self-awareness ...

5. Nature and Dragon Nature

Extract from a lecture given in Dornach on
30 September 1923

*In this passage Steiner refers to the perception which
ancient people had of Michael and the dragon, relating
this to its significance for human beings today. He
describes the dragon in more detail as a being who desired
his own will and intelligence in opposition to cosmic laws;
his expulsion from a world of spirit is a descent into a
denser form of existence, ultimately taking up residence
(Steiner elsewhere refers to this as his 'fortress') in the
human being. Nature outside us is a pure reflection of
cosmic laws, while our capacity for self-awareness means
that instinctive forces of desire become conscious in us,
leading to a 'fall' from innocence. If we do not make
conscious efforts to oppose such drives and desires,
therefore, nature becomes an ugly force in us – the dragon
in fact.*

The modern view of man's origin looks back into
the past to find beings less and less human, less
spiritual, from whom we are descended. In earlier

times people traced back the evolution of mankind to ever more spiritual conditions of existence than prevail today. They looked back to a pre-earthly condition when the present human form did not as yet exist, a time when beings lived in a finer, less material environment than that which now surrounds and forms us. These beings were more 'spiritual' than the people of today.

Of such a nature was the dragon being whom Michael fights. He was destined one day, in a later age, to assume human form, but he must bide his time. The time did not depend on him but on the decree of spiritual beings who stood above him. Until that time he was to remain entirely within the will of these higher beings. But before his hour was come, pride grew in him. He wanted to have his own will at a time when he should still have been living in the higher will, and therefore he stood in opposition to it. Independence of will was only possible to such beings in a denser matter than then existed. If they persisted in opposition they must inevitably change and become different beings. This being found it impossible to continue to live in the same spirituality. His fellow beings found his existence in their realm disturbing, even destructive. Michael felt it so. Michael had remained in the will of the higher spiritual beings. He undertook to compel the opposing being to assume the only form possible for an independent will at that stage of the world's evolution, to assume animal form, that of the dragon or serpent. Higher animal forms had not yet made their appearance. This 'dragon' was not, of course, materially visible, but supersensible.

Such was the soul-picture a person of earlier times had of the fight of Michael with the dragon. For him it was a fact that had taken place before there was nature visible to the human eye, before the human being even existed in his present form.

The world we know originated in the world in which this event took place. The kingdom into which the dragon was driven has become 'nature', has assumed material form and become visible to the senses. It is, as it were, a deposit of the earlier world. The realm in which Michael has preserved his spirit-devoted will has remained 'above' — purified like a liquid from which a substance once contained in solution has been deposited. It is a realm that must continue to remain invisible to the senses.

Nature, however, considered apart from the human being, has not succumbed to the dragon. The power of the dragon was not strong enough to manifest visibly in nature, but remained in her as an invisible spirit. The dragon had to sunder his being from nature, which had become a mirror of the higher spirituality from which he had fallen.

Into this world the human being was placed. He was able to participate in nature and in the higher spirituality. He thus became a kind of double being. In nature itself the dragon remained powerless. In nature as it comes to life in the human being he retains his power. The nature human beings receive into themselves lives in them as desire, as animal drives and lust. And this made possible the 'Fall of man'.

The adversary has found his abode in the human being. Michael has remained true to his own being. If we turn to Michael with that part of our life which originates from higher spirituality, then the inward fight of Michael and the dragon arises in the soul ...

The time when autumn approaches must inevitably recall this fight with the dragon ... That picture was dimmed when nature and with her the dragon was more powerful. But with the oncoming frost it appears again before the soul. And this picture is a reality. It is as if a curtain enclosing the warmth of summer were drawn back, revealing the world of spirit. We partake in the life of the year, we go with it in its course; but it enmeshes us in that kingdom where the 'adversary' sets his invisible power within us as ugliness against nature's beauty.

With the beginning of autumn appears the spirit of 'strength in beauty' when nature hides her beauty, driving the adversary too into concealment. It was with thoughts and feelings such as these that people of ancient times kept the festival of Michael in their hearts.

The picture of Michael's fight with the dragon expresses a strong awareness that we must direct and guide our inner life of soul in a way that nature cannot. Our modern thinking is inclined to distrust such an idea. We are afraid of becoming estranged from nature. We want to enjoy her in all her beauty, to revel in her abundance of life, and are loath to let ourselves be robbed of this enjoyment by contemplating nature's fall from the spiritual. In our striving for knowledge, moreover, we want to let the natural, material world speak. We fear to lose ourselves in all kinds of fantasy if we allow the spirit, which transcends the perception of external nature, to play a part in our striving for knowledge about the essential reality of the world ...

The festival of a consciousness which is self-aware, which brings us close to our true humanity, is present when the leaves are falling. We only need to become conscious of it. It is the festival of Michael, the festival of autumn's onset. The picture of 'Michael triumphant' can live in us. In summer we are embraced lovingly by nature; but if we are not to be deprived of our own centre and balance, we must not lose ourselves entirely in her but be able to rise up in autumn to strengthen the spiritual nature of our own being.

6. The Michael Imagination

Extract from a lecture given in Dornach on
5 October 1923

This lecture starts with a riddle and ends with the riddle's answer. But in the space between question and answer Steiner expands a vivid pictorial imagination of Michael and the dragon, drawn as he says from a perception of actual processes and warring energies that constitute us and the wider universe. In doing so he touches briefly on the whole nature of art and imagination. As artists — or poets, or musicians — do we merely create arbitrary 'figments' and fantasies, or can our artistic perception be informed by reality? Michael, as a being intrinsically faithful to cosmic law, awaits our efforts to raise ourselves to the truth of art and the art of truth.

Today I would like to begin by reminding you how events that take place behind the veil of appearances, outside the physical, sense-perceptible world, can be described in pictorial terms. One has to speak in this way of such events, but the pictures wholly correspond to reality.

As far as sense-perceptible events are concerned, we live at a time of hard tests for humanity, and these tests will become harder still. Many old forms of civilization to which people still mistakenly cling will sink into the abyss, and humanity will be fiercely urged to find its way through to something new. In speaking of the course that external events will take in the near future we cannot—as I have often said—feel any sense of optimism. But we cannot form a valid judgement of the significance of external events without also considering the cosmic events that determine and direct them behind the veil of the senses.

If we look attentively at our surroundings with our physical eyes and other senses we perceive the physical environment of the earth and the various kingdoms of nature within it. This is the environment in which all kinds of wind and weather manifest in the course of the year. We have all this before us when we direct our senses towards the outer world. These are the external facts. But behind the atmosphere, the sun-illumined atmosphere, lies another world, perceptible by spiritual organs as we may call them. Compared with the sense-world, this other world is a higher world, one in which a kind of spiritual or astral light, in which spiritual existence and spiritual deeds shine out and run their course. And these, truly, are no less significant for the whole evolution of the world and humanity than historical events taking place in the earth's external, physical environment.

Anyone who can penetrate these astral realms nowadays, wandering through them as one may wander among woods and mountains and find signposts at crossroads, may find 'signposts' there in the astral light, inscribed in spiritual script. But these signposts have a quite special characteristic; they are not comprehensible without further explanation, even for someone who can 'read' in the astral light. In the spiritual world and its communications things are not made as easy and accessible as possible. Anything encountered there presents itself as a riddle to be solved. Only through inner investigation, through inwardly experiencing the riddle and much else, can one discover the meaning of an inscription on a spiritual signpost.

Thus at this time — in fact for some decades now, but particularly at this time of hard trials for humanity — one can read in the astral light a remarkable saying. Just as we find directions to help us on our way — even in romantic landscapes — so, however prosaic it sounds, we encounter an important spiritual signpost in the astral light. Time and again, repeated in the same way, we find the following saying inscribed in spiritual script of great significance:

O humanity,
you form it to serve you,
you reveal its material worth
in many of your works.
Yet it will only make you sound and whole
when is revealed to you
its spirit's lofty power.

Injunctions of this kind that point to facts significant
for humanity are inscribed, as I have said, in the
astral light. They present themselves first as a kind
of riddle to be solved, so that human beings may
activate their soul forces. Today we will contribute
something to the solving of the riddle contained in
this verse—actually a simple riddle, but a vitally
important one for human beings today.

Let us recall that many of our studies here have
been concerned with the course of the year. Initially
one can observe the seasons quite externally. When
spring comes we see nature sprouting and budding,
plants growing and coming into flower. We see life
springing up everywhere from the soil. All this
increases as summer draws on, rising to its highest
level of activity. Then when autumn comes it
withers and fades, dying back in winter into the lap
of the earth ...

But we can continually deepen our sympathetic
participation in the course of the year, can enrich it

so that we do not live, you can say, constrained within our skin, letting the outer world pass us by. On the contrary we can enrich our experience so that we feel ourselves living in the blossoming of every flower, in the breaking open of buds, in that wonderful secret of the morning, the glistening of dewdrops in the rays of the sun ...

Today, generally speaking, people feel they can enter into the life of nature only in the season of growth—of germination, budding, flowering and fruiting. Even if they cannot fully experience all this, they have more sympathy and perception for it than they have for the autumnal season of wilting and fading. But in fact we can only earn the right to enter fully into the growth of spring if we can also enter into the time when summer wanes and autumn draws on—the season of sinking and dying that comes with winter. And if, during high summer, we rise inwardly in cosmic waking sleep, with the elemental beings,[6] to the region where planetary activity in the outer world can be inwardly experienced,[7] then we ought equally to sink ourselves down under the frost and snow mantle of winter, so that we enter into the secrets of the womb of the earth during midwinter. And we ought, too, to participate in nature's fading and dying as autumn begins.

If we are to participate in nature's waning, as we

do in her growth, we can only do so if in a certain sense we can experience nature's dying in our inner being. For if we become more sensitive to the secret workings of nature, and thus participate actively in nature's germinating and fruiting, it follows that we will also lovingly experience the effects of autumn in the external world. But it would bring us no comfort if we were to experience this only in the form it takes in nature, if we were to come to a nature consciousness of the secrets of autumn and winter in the same way as we do of the secrets of spring and summer. When autumn and winter draw on, when Michaelmas arrives, we certainly must enter sensitively into the processes of fading and dying. But we must not, as we do in summer, give ourselves over wholly to nature consciousness. On the contrary we must then devote ourselves to self-awareness. When outer nature is dying we must oppose nature consciousness with consciousness of self.

Then the form of Michael stands before us. If, guided by anthroposophy, we enter fully into consciousness of nature but also awaken in ourselves an autumnal consciousness of self, then the image of Michael and the dragon will stand majestically before us, revealing pictorially how nature consciousness is overcome by consciousness of self when autumn draws near. This will happen if we can experience not only an inner spring and summer but also a dying, death-bringing autumn and winter. This will make it possible for the picture of Michael and the dragon to appear again as a powerful imagination, summoning us to inner activity.

For those of us who wrestle our way through to a living experience of this picture, it expresses something very powerful. For when, following St John's Tide, July, August and September draw on, we become aware of how we have been living through a waking sleep of inner planetary experience together with the earth's elemental beings, and we come to realize what this signifies.

It signifies an inner process of combustion, but we must not imagine this like external combustion. All the processes that take a definite form in the outer world also occur within the human organism, but in a different guise. And so it is a fact that inner processes within us reflect the year's changing seasons.

The inner process which occurs during high summer is a permeation of the organism by what manifests as sulphur in the material world of substance. When we live with the summer sun and its effects we experience a sulphurizing process in our physical and etheric[8] being. The sulphur which we bear within us as a useful substance has a special importance for us in high summer, one quite different from that at other seasons of the year. It becomes a kind of combustion process. In us, at midsummer, sulphur naturally rises to a specially enhanced condition. Material substances in different beings conceal secrets not dreamt of by materialistic science.

Everything in us that is physical and etheric in nature is thus warmed through at midsummer with inward sulphur fire, to use Jacob Boehme's expression.[9] It is a gentle, intimate process, not perceptible by ordinary consciousness, but—as is generally true of other such processes—it has a tremendous, decisive significance for events in the cosmos.

This sulphurizing process in human bodies at midsummer, despite being so delicate and imperceptible to us, has a great importance for cosmic evolution. A great deal happens out there in the cosmos when in summer human beings shine inwardly with the enhanced sulphur process at work in them. At the same time as physically visible glow-worms shine out around St John's day, our inner being also starts to shine when viewed spiritually from out in the cosmos, becoming visible as light to the etheric eyes of other cosmic beings. That is the sulphurizing process. At the height of summer human beings begin to shine out into cosmic space as brightly for other cosmic beings as glow-worms shine with their own light in the meadows of midsummer.

Seen from the cosmos this is a majestically beautiful sight, for human beings shine out into the cosmos in glorious astral light during high summer. But at the same time it gives ahrimanic[10] powers the opportunity to draw close to humanity. These ahrimanic powers are closely related to the sulphurizing process in the human organism. We can see, on the one hand, how human beings shine out into the cosmos in the St John's light and, on the other, how the dragon-like, serpentine forms of Ahriman wind their way among human beings shining in the astral light, trying to ensnare and embrace them, to draw them down into the realm of semi-conscious sleep and dreams. There, caught in a web of illusion, human beings would become enchanted dreamers, and in this condition would be prey to ahrimanic powers. All this is significant for the cosmos also.

And when in high summer, from a particular constellation, meteors fall in great showers of cosmic iron, then this cosmic iron, which contains an enormously healing force, is the weapon which the gods bring to bear against Ahriman, as he seeks dragon-like to coil around the shining human forms. The force falling to earth in meteoric iron is truly a cosmic force through which the higher gods strive for victory over the ahrimanic powers as autumn approaches. And this majestic display in cosmic space, when the August meteor showers stream down upon the human being shining in the astral light, has its counterpart—so delicate and apparently very small—in a change that occurs in the human blood. This human blood, which in truth is not such a material thing as modern science imagines but is permeated by soul and spiritual impulses, is rayed through by the force which is carried as iron into the blood, waging war there on anxiety, fear and hatred. The processes set in motion in every blood corpuscle when the iron shoots into it are the same, on a minute scale, as those which take place when meteors fall in a shining stream through the air. This permeation of human blood by the fear-dispelling force of iron is a meteoric activity. The effect of iron's influx is to drive fear and anxiety out of the blood.

And so, while the gods with their meteors wage war on the spirit who desires to radiate fear over all the earth through his coiling, serpent-like form, and as they cause iron to stream radiantly into this fear-tainted atmosphere, which reaches its peak when autumn approaches or when summer wanes—so the same process occurs inwardly in human beings when their blood is permeated with iron. We can understand these things only if, on the one hand, we understand their spiritual significance and, on the other, if we recognize how the sulphur process and the iron process in human beings are connected with corresponding events in the cosmos.

Those who look out into space and see a shooting star should say, with reverence for the gods: 'That phenomenon in the great breadths of space has its continuous, minute counterpart within me. Out there are the shooting stars while in every one of my blood corpuscles iron is taking form. My life is full of shooting stars, miniature shooting stars.' And this inner fall of shooting stars, this activity in the blood, is especially important when autumn approaches, when the sulphur process is at its peak. When human beings are shining like glow-worms in the way I described, then the counter-force is also present, for millions of tiny meteors are scintillating inwardly in their blood. This is the connection between the inner human being and the universe. And then we can see how, especially when autumn approaches, the nervous system rays out sulphur towards the brain. The whole person can then be seen, as it were, as a sulphur-illumined phantom.[11]

But raying into this bluish-yellow sulphur atmosphere come the blood's meteor swarms. That is the other phantom. While the sulphur phantom rises in clouds from our lower parts towards our head, the iron-forming process rays out from our heads, pouring itself like a stream of meteors into the life of the blood. That is the other phantom. While the sulphur phantom rises in clouds from our lower parts towards our head, the iron-forming process rays out from our heads, pouring itself like a stream of meteors into the life of the blood.

Such are human beings when Michaelmas draws near. We must learn to make conscious use of the meteoric forces in our blood. We must learn to keep the Michael festival by making it a festival for the conquest of anxiety and fear, a festival of inner strength and initiative—a festival for the commemoration of selfless self-awareness.

Just as we celebrate the Redeemer's birth at Christmas, his death and resurrection at Easter, and at St John's the outpouring of human souls into cosmic space, so at Michaelmas—if the Michaelmas festival is to be rightly understood—we must celebrate what lives spiritually in the sulphurizing and meteorizing process in human beings. Especially at Michaelmas we should grow aware of the whole soul-spiritual significance of human consciousness. Then we will be able to say to ourselves: 'I will become master of this process, which otherwise just takes its natural course outside my awareness if—just as I feel deep gratitude before Christ's birth at Christmas and have a profound inner response to

Easter—I now learn to experience how, during this autumn festival of Michael, there should grow in me all that counters love of ease, and anxiety, and makes for the unfolding of inner initiative and free, strong, courageous will.' The festival of strong will: that is how we should conceive of the Michael festival. If that is done, if knowledge of nature becomes true, spiritual human consciousness of self, then the Michael festival will shine out in its true colours.

But before human beings can think of celebrating the Michael festival there will have to be a renewal in human souls. It is the renewal of the whole human disposition of heart and soul that should be celebrated at Michaelmas—not as an outward or conventional ceremony, but as a festival which renews us wholly and inwardly.

Then, out of all I have described, the majestic image of Michael and the dragon will arise once more. But this picture of Michael and the dragon paints itself out of the cosmos. The dragon paints itself for us, forming its body out of bluish-yellow sulphur streams. We see the dragon shaping itself in shimmering clouds of radiance out of the sulphur vapours; and over the dragon rises the figure of Michael—Michael with his sword.

We shall picture this rightly only if we see the space where Michael displays his power and his lordship over the dragon as filled not with nebulous clouds but with showers of meteoric iron. These showers take form from the power that streams out from Michael's heart. They are welded together into the sword of Michael, who overcomes the dragon with his sword of meteoric iron.

If we understand what is going on in the universe and in human beings, then the cosmos paints images in us out of its own innate forces. Then in our paintings we will not lay on this or that colour according to arbitrary human ideas, but will paint, in harmony with divine powers, the world that expresses their being, the whole being of Michael and the dragon as it can hover before us. Ancient pictures and images can be renewed if we can paint in this way out of direct contemplation of the cosmos. Then our pictures will show what is really there, and not what fanciful individuals may portray more arbitrarily in images of Michael and the dragon.

Then humanity will come to understand these things and to reflect on them with understanding, and will bring mind and feeling and will to meet the autumn months. Then, at the beginning of autumn, at the Michael festival, the picture of Michael with the dragon will stand there to act as a powerful summons, a powerful spur to action, which must work on human beings in the midst of the events of our times. And then we shall understand how this impulse points symbolically to something in which the whole destiny and perhaps indeed the whole tragedy of our epoch is being played out.

During the last three or four centuries we have developed a magnificent science and extensive technology, using the most widespread substance to be found on earth. We have learned to use iron to make nearly all the most essential and important things produced by mankind in a materialistic age. In our locomotives, factories, everywhere, we have developed a whole material civilization based on iron or steel (which is transformed iron). And all the uses to which iron is put are a symbolic picture of how we have built our whole life and outlook on matter, and wish to go on doing so. But this is a descending, declining path. We can rescue ourselves from impending dangers only if we start to spiritualize life in this very domain where iron is used, if we penetrate through what surrounds it to the spiritual. We must turn from the iron which is used for making engines and look up again to the meteoric iron which showers down from the cosmos to the earth and is the outer material from which the power of Michael is forged. Humanity must come to see the great significance of the following words: 'Here on earth, in the materialistic age, you have made use of iron, based on insights gained from your observation of matter. Just as you must transform your vision of matter by developing natural science into spiritual science, so you must rise from your former idea of iron to a perception of meteoric iron, the iron of Michael's sword. Then healing will come from what you can make of it.'

> O humanity,
> you form it to serve you,
> you reveal its material worth
> in many of your works.
> Yet it will only make you sound and whole
> when is revealed to you
> its spirit's lofty power.

In other words, the lofty power of Michael, with the sword he has welded from meteoric iron in cosmic space. Healing will come when our material civilization proves capable of spiritualizing the power of iron into the power of Michael iron, which gives human beings consciousness of self instead of nature consciousness.

MICHAEL, SPIRIT OF OUR AGE

7. The Signs of Michael

Extract from a lecture given in Dornach on
13 January 1924

*This lecture explores the nature of Michael in greater
depth, as the presiding spirit of our age. He leaves the
human being free, awaiting his actions and their consequences, and yet at the same time fiercely – though
silently – opposing everything of a socially divisive and
nationalistic character, everything that grows fixed and
impermeable to the spirit such as our written and printed
words. Here again the idea of a deeper 'reading' and
'writing' surfaces.*

The Michael period, which the world entered
already in the last third of the nineteenth century
and into which human beings will have to enter
with ever-increasing consciousness, is very different from former Michael epochs. Each of the
seven great archangel spirits exert their separate
influences in different epochs on mankind's earthly
evolution. Thus, after given periods of time, the
guidance of Gabriel, Uriel, Raphael or Michael is

repeated. Our own age is however essentially different from a former Michael epoch. Since the first third of the fifteenth century, the human being now stands in a quite different relationship to the world of spirit than he ever did before. This new connection to the world of spirit also determines the very particular kind of relationship we have with the spirit now guiding the destiny of mankind, whom we may call by the ancient name of Michael ...

Since the beginning of the Michael epoch, since the end of the 1870s ... we no longer need that other condition of clairvoyance attained in a semiconscious way ... We may say that the old Rosicrucian movement is characterized by the fact that its most illumined minds had an intense longing to meet Michael, but could only do so in the realms of dream. Since the end of the last third of the nineteenth century, however, human beings can meet Michael in the spirit in a fully conscious way.

But Michael is a being who reveals nothing if we do not bring him something from our diligent spiritual work on earth. Michael is a silent spirit — silent and taciturn. Other ruling spirits are loquacious — in a spiritual sense of course — but Michael is taciturn, and speaks very little. At most he will give sparing indications, for he does not communicate with us so much through the words as, if I may so express it, through his gaze, the power and direction of his gaze.

This is because Michael concerns himself most of all with what human beings create out of the spirit. He lives with the consequences of all that humanity creates. The other spirits live more with the causes, whereas Michael lives more with the consequences. The other spirits kindle in man the impulses for what he should do. Michael is the true spiritual hero of freedom. He leaves human beings free to act, then takes the results of their deeds and carries them on and out into the cosmos, to continue in the cosmos what human beings themselves cannot yet achieve.

We can have the feeling about other beings of the hierarchy of the archangels that they give us the impulses to do this or that. To a greater or lesser degree such impulses derive from them. Michael on the other hand is the spirit from whom no impulses come, initially. Characteristic of his dawning period of rulership is that things occur out of human freedom. But when a person does something out of spiritual activity or inner freedom, consciously or unconsciously kindled by reading the astral light,[12] then Michael carries the human earthly deed out into the cosmos so that it becomes cosmic deed. Michael cares for the results of human actions, while the other spirits care for the causes.

However Michael is not only a silent, taciturn spirit. He meets us with a very clear gesture of rejection for many things which the human being of today still holds firmly to. For example, all knowledge about human, animal or plant life which lays stress on inherited characteristics — on everything to do with physical inheritance — is, we feel, repelled and rejected by Michael. He means to show by this that such knowledge is no help to us in the world of spirit. Only what we discover in the human, animal and plant kingdoms that is independent of purely hereditary nature can be lifted towards Michael. Then we receive not the eloquent gesture of rejection but the look of agreement which tells us that it is a fitting thought, one acceptable to cosmic guidance. For this is what we learn increasingly to strive for, to meditate in such a way that we strike through to the astral light and see the secrets of existence, and then come before Michael and receive his approving look which tells us: 'That is right, that is in accordance with cosmic guidance.'

Michael also sternly rejects all divisive elements such as human languages. So long as we only clothe our knowledge in language's outer garb, rather than lifting it right up into the realm of thinking, we cannot approach Michael. In the spiritual world today, therefore, a highly significant battle is taking place. For on the one hand the Michael impulse has entered humanity's evolution, is at work there. But on the other hand there is still much in humanity that will not receive this Michael impulse, that wishes to reject it—nationalistic feelings, for example, which flared up in the nineteenth century and became strong in the twentieth, stronger and stronger. The principle of nationalism has ordered, or rather disordered, many things in recent times. Disordered is truly the right word for it.

All this is in terrible opposition to the Michael principle. All this contains ahrimanic forces[13] which strive against the influence and impulse of Michael forces upon human life. One can witness this battle: the ahrimanic spirits storming upwards, trying to bear upwards what results from principles of inherited nationality—which Michael sternly rejects and repels.

A fierce spiritual conflict is truly taking place in our time, for a large proportion of humanity thinks only in words, not in real thoughts; and to think only in words is no way to Michael. We only approach Michael when we get through the words to real inner experiences of the spirit—when we do not hang on the words but arrive at real inner, spiritual experience.

This is the very essence, the secret of modern initiation: to get beyond words to a living experience of the spiritual. It is not contrary to a feeling for the beauty of language. Precisely when we no longer *think* in language we begin to *feel* it.[14] We begin to have it streaming in us and out from us as an element of feeling. That however is something that people today must still strive for. Perhaps, to begin with, they cannot attain it in speech, but through handwriting. For it must be said that people today do not own their handwriting, but are mastered by it. What does this mean? It means that in our wrist, in our hand, we have a certain way of writing. We write mechanically, compelled by the hand. This is something that fetters us. We only become unfettered when we write as we paint or draw — when every letter beside the next becomes something drawn:

Goetheanum

Then there is no longer what is ordinarily called 'handwriting'. Instead we draw the form of the letter. Our relationship to the letter becomes objective, and we observe its form.

For this reason, strange as it may sound, learning to write was prohibited in certain Rosicrucian schools until the age of 14 or 15, so that the form, the mechanism which comes to expression in writing, did not enter the human organism. Pupils were only introduced to the form of letters once their faculty of observation had developed. Then at the same time as learning the conventional letters needed for human communication, they had to learn others — specifically Rosicrucian letters — which are regarded nowadays as a secret script. They were not intended as such. The idea was that for an *A* one should learn another sign at the same time, ☉, so that one was not fettered to one sign only. By this means one could free oneself from signs altogether, and feel the real *A* as something greater than its mere sign. Otherwise the mere symbol *A* would become too closely identified with the living, floating, weaving sound of Ah[15] that sounds forth from us.

In actual fact nothing hinders us more from writing in the astral light than ordinary writing. This artificial and fixed way of rendering experience is a great hindrance to reading in the astral light. One must always first overcome the obstacle of ordinary writing when one wants to read in the astral light.

This leads me back to something else which I mentioned some while ago. In developing spiritual knowledge one must always be present with full, inner activity. I have many notebooks in which I write or draw the results and findings I come to. I generally do not look at them again. Yet by calling into activity not only the head but the whole human being, knowledge and perceptions come forth which take hold of you. Whoever adopts this process gradually accustoms himself not to care so much for what is seen physically, which is already fixed, but to remain in the activity so as not to spoil his faculty of perceiving in the astral light. It is good, therefore, when you fix things in ordinary script, to hold back from close identification with the script itself — either by 'drawing' the letters in an artistic way as though painting them, or by not looking back at what you have written. Only then can we acquire the faculty of preserving for ourselves the impressions of the astral light.

If we are obliged to relate ourselves to writing in the modern way we mar our spiritual progress. For this reason great care is taken in our Waldorf educational method to protect the human being from such an extreme exposure to writing as is current in today's educational approach. Care is taken to enable the human being to continue to inhabit the realm of spirit, for that is necessary.

The world must once more take up the initiation principle and integrate it with other principles at work in civilization. Only then will human beings be able to acquire something in their souls with which they can go to meet Michael, encountering Michael's approving gaze which says: 'That is in accordance with the cosmos.' Then the will is strengthened and made robust, and the human being is integrated into the world's spiritual evolution. Then we ourselves work in harmony with the impulses which Michael aims to instil into human and earthly evolution in the Michael age now beginning ...

8. The Dawn of a Michael Age

Extract from a lecture given in Dornach on
28 July 1924

*In this brief extract Steiner touches on the nature of the
new Michael age in contrast to the previous age of Gabriel
when physical existence was humanity's rightful
cornerstone. It no longer is, but the past fights with all
tenacity to keep its hold on us, and we can experience the
great conflict between nationalist and/or materialist
movements of all kinds and a new, more globally aware
consciousness. There are of course two sides to globali-
zation: one which spreads materialism across the globe,
and another which seeks the universally human in people
of all cultures. In response to Steiner's reference to the
end of the twentieth century we have to ask ourselves,
painfully, whether Michael is still waiting empty-handed,
and whether people from very different backgrounds and
movements as yet do enough to reach out to one another.*

We know that the age of darkness led eventually to
that condition of the human soul which entirely
closed human eyes of spirit to perception of the

supersensible world. We know that in ancient times of human evolution it was a common condition of mankind to see into the world of spirit, albeit in a dreamlike and more or less instinctive way. To doubt the reality of the world of spirit was utterly impossible in olden times. But if that ancient condition had continued, if mankind had lived on in that instinctive wisdom and spiritual vision, what we may call human intelligence would never have developed — personal use and mastery of the intellect or reasoning faculty by individual human beings. And as we know, this is connected with the capacity for free will. The one is unthinkable without the other. Thus in that dim, instinctive condition that once belonged to mankind, in which human beings experienced the ever-present world of spirit, they could neither attain freedom nor that independence of thinking which we can call the use of intelligence by single individuals. The time had to come for these two things: free, personal use of intelligence, and freedom of the human will. Hence human consciousness had to lose the original, instinctive vision that penetrated the world of spirit. All this has now been accomplished. Though it is not quite clear to every single individual, yet it has been accomplished for humanity in general. With the close of the nineteenth century, the dark age — which darkened the world of spirit yet opened up for human beings the use of intelligence and free will—had run its course. We are now entering upon an age when we must once again be touched by the reality of the world of spirit.

True, we cannot say that this age has begun in a very light-filled way. It is as though the first decades of the twentieth century have brought over humanity all the evil ever previously experienced by mankind. And yet despite this, it has now become possible, as a general principle within evolution, to reach the light of spiritual life. It is only through a kind of inertia that people have persisted in the habits of the age of darkness. They have perpetuated these habits in the twentieth century. And because the light can now arise again, illumining the truth, these habits from the age of darkness have come forth in a far more evil form than was possible in Kali Yuga[16] when they were justified . . .

Thus for about three centuries before the end of the 1870s there was what we may call the dominion of Gabriel. For those who study human evolution, not superficially as is common today, but in a profounder way, this rulership of Gabriel is expressed in the fact that the deepest and most important impulses at work in humanity during that period were implanted in what we call the forces of heredity. Never were the forces of physical inheritance so important as in the three centuries preceding the last third of the nineteenth century.

Let us observe how this expressed itself. We know that in the nineteenth century issues relating to heredity came to dominate human awareness. People felt that their qualities of soul and spirit were dependent on heredity. It was as though, at the last moment, they came to feel what had been holding sway in human evolution as a real law of nature in the sixteenth, seventeenth and eighteenth centuries, and on into a great part of the nineteenth century.

During this period the qualities associated with physical reproduction became especially important. Again we find an outward sign of this fact in the great interest in reproduction and all sexual matters that was felt at the end of the nineteenth century. In the centuries I have referred to, the most important spiritual impulses did indeed approach humanity in this way, seeking realization through physical inheritance.

Now the age in which Michael leads and guides humanity will stand in complete contrast to this . . . An age of Michael is characterized by many different conditions, but especially by the fact that the most spiritual interests of humanity become predominant. In such an age especially, a cosmopolitan, international character will permeate the world. National divisions and distinctions cease to be important.

It was above all in the age of Gabriel that national impulses within European civilization, with its American offshoot, became so firmly rooted. In our age of Michael, over the next three centuries, such national impulses will be completely superseded. This is the case in every Michael age; a common feature runs through all humanity, something of a universally human character, as opposed to the narrower interests of single groups or nations ...

My dear friends, the anthroposophist should receive these things into his awareness. He should understand that he is already called, now, to prepare that spirituality which must continually spread and develop until the culmination is reached at the end of the twentieth century ... the true anthroposophist must be conscious of the need to participate in the battle between Michael and Ahriman. Only when a spirituality such as now seeks to flow through the anthroposophical movement unites with other spiritual streams and movements will Michael find the impulses which unite him once more with the intelligence that has grown earthly but still truly belongs to him.

It still remains my task to show you by what refined and clever means Ahriman is seeking to hinder this,[17] to show you how sharp is the conflict that rages in our twentieth century. Through all these things we can become aware of the earnestness of our time and of the courage needed for us to take our rightful place within these spiritual streams.

9. Michaelic Thinking

Extract from a lecture given in Dornach on
23 November 1919

*The references to Asia and America in the penultimate
sentence of the following passage strike one as prophetic.
Again Steiner highlights the conflicts raging around
contemporary humanity, and our doomed efforts to deal
with a new evolutionary situation by reaching for past —
and therefore impotent — remedies. But perhaps the most
striking, revelatory and even shocking idea in this extract
is the simple and profound thought that in some true
sense we are invisible — a real seed-thought for a more
spiritual age.*

Let me characterize this Michaelic thinking more
precisely. When you encounter a fellow human
being today, your conscious impression is really an
entirely materialistic one. You tell yourself (not
aloud of course, and perhaps not even as a conscious
thought, but at a deeper level of awareness), 'This is a
person made of flesh and blood, composed of
earthly substances.' And you say the same of

animals and plants. But this attitude is justified only in so far as the mineral substances you encounter in a human being or animal are concerned.

Let us take the most extreme case, human beings, and examine them purely in terms of their external form [Steiner draws on blackboard]. You do not really 'see' the outer form, as this outer form is more than 90 per cent fluid. What your physical eyes perceive is the mineral element that fills out the structure. You see whatever the person has absorbed from the outer, mineral world. You do not see the being who did this absorption, who united with the mineral element. Hence, when we encounter another human being we speak correctly only if we say to ourselves: 'What stands before me are material particles that this individual's spirit form has stored and gathered, thereby making something invisible visible.'

Actual human beings are invisible, truly invisible. All of you sitting here listening to this lecture are invisible to physical senses. But a certain number of shapes with a certain capacity to attract particles of matter are sitting here [drawing], and these particles are visible. We see only the mineral element in people; the real individuals sitting here are supersensible beings, and hence invisible.

Michaelic thinking brings us to full consciousness of this in every moment of our waking lives ...

[We must] familiarize ourselves with the super-sensible in the immediate world of the senses, that is to say in the world of human beings, animals and plants. This is the path of Michael. Its continuation is to find the Christ impulse in this world we recognize as supersensible.

In telling you this I am describing the deepest impulses underlying the social issues of our time. The abstract League of Nations[18] is not going to solve international problems. The abstractions it offers won't bring people together. But the spirit beings about whom we have been speaking, who guide us to supersensible realms, will do so.

Outwardly, modern humanity faces hard struggles. No economic or spiritual remedies are available from the pharmacy of past historical evolution to help us face such serious battles, which are only beginning, and which will lead the out-moded, worn-out evolutionary impulses they stem from to absurdity. The ferments that have brought Europe to the edge of the abyss, that will pit Asia and America against each other, engendering worldwide conflicts, are products of the past. The path of human evolution to absurdity may be countered only by travelling the path that leads to the spirit: the Michael path, which becomes the path of Christ.

10. The Michael Impulse and the Mystery of Golgotha

Extract from a lecture given in Stuttgart on
20 May 1913

Touching here on the central significance to our evolution of Christ's death at Golgotha, and on Michael's role as messenger and 'countenance' of Christ, Steiner also makes a plea here for us to develop greater, more accurate discernment in the spiritual realm rather than a vaguely 'spiritual' attitude. We can hone our sense-free perceptions now in a way previously impossible, because of the 'spiritual tidal wave' now flowing towards us in the Michael age.

We have tried to throw some light on the character of our modern age as governed by cosmic law. This is something we should not pass over lightly. For when we speak of the spiritual forces, the spiritual influences of a particular age, these are likewise the forces and impulses at work in the soul of each one of us. We cannot live in harmony with our own souls unless we develop the right relationship to these forces and influences at work in our times ...

In my last lecture I endeavoured to show that at the present time we are living in what one may call the Michael age. An understanding for spiritual things is now becoming possible for an increasing number of souls. During the course of previous centuries it was possible to acquire an understanding above all of things shown by external science, of physical, chemical and physiological laws, of everything related to external space and time. During the Gabriel age understanding awoke for the onward march of scientific advances, everything that inclined people to a scientific view of the world. Now, however, we are entering an age in which it will be equally possible to understand things of the spirit.

At no time in human evolution have two successive epochs been so radically different from one another as that which has just run its course and the epoch which we are now entering. And never before have human souls been more alien to one another than will be the souls of those who incline towards the spiritual and those who adhere still to what developed in past centuries. Nor will it be long before those who believe they stand firmly rooted in the truths of materialism are quite at odds with those who longingly seek for an understanding of spiritual worlds. Since the last third of the nineteenth century a spiritual tidal wave from higher worlds has been flowing into our world, and has made it possible for us to understand the way in which human and world evolution are spiritually guided.

Nearly two thousand years ago the event took place which you all know as the Mystery of Golgotha, which we have often referred to. We have looked at it from many different angles and have found it to be the centre of gravity of all human evolution. I believe it has become quite clear that, irrespective of any religious views or creeds, based purely on the science of spirit itself it is possible to understand this event and share our understanding with advocates of every shade of religious belief ...

In times when people stood nearer to the spiritual they had a feeling of reverence for the divinity in which we live and move and have our being, whose name it is not always right to utter. And for that reason the ancient Hebrews, in order not to utter the name, used the expression the 'Countenance of Jehovah'. The human being's countenance is what he turns outwards, which expresses and reveals his inner nature. It is not the whole of his being. One knows a person as he is in his inner being by the features of his countenance, but one does not therefore presume to speak of the whole person when referring to his face.

At that time therefore, Michael was called the 'Countenance of Jehovah'. People preferred to speak of the representative through whom Yahweh revealed himself to mankind as though through an external countenance. Even in intimate circles they preferred to name the representative than speak the name of Yahweh himself. Michael was at that time regarded as the spiritual regent of the age, as Yahweh's messenger, as the member of the hierarchies from whom streamed forth the impulse that was to bring about an understanding of the event of Golgotha.

In the intervening centuries other beings from the ranks of the archangels have guided humanity's spiritual evolution. But the one who guided it when preparation was underway for the Mystery of Golgotha is the same being who is now sending a flood of supersensible life into the world of the senses. There was a Michael age then, and a new Michael age is now beginning. There is however a huge difference between the previous Michael age and our own.

It would take us too far today to describe the kind of understanding people have been able to bring to the Mystery of Golgotha during the period which elapsed between that former Michael age and ours.

There have been deeply fervent souls whose intense need for belief has enabled them to gain a relationship with the Mystery of Golgotha and its central bearer. There have been profoundly religious natures all through the centuries since the Mystery of Golgotha, down to our own times. But although the Mystery of Golgotha exists as a real fact at the beginning of modern times, human souls cannot, nevertheless, presume to understand it fully without preparation. New epochs will succeed one another in which human souls grow ever deeper and develop an increasing understanding of what happened at the Mystery of Golgotha. The event itself stands there as a great turning point in human evolution, and understanding of it will continue to grow and ripen throughout the earth's spiritual evolution. We cannot engrave this deeply enough into our souls.

Let us draw on a certain metaphysical abstraction to examine what actually took place at that time. We have described it from various points of view. Let us now choose a more abstract approach, but one which, if we allow it to work on us, can call forth a deep feeling in our souls.

When we study the things around us using ordinary thinking and even scientific powers of observation, we can learn to know nature's laws in the mineral, plant, animal and human kingdoms. These laws all culminate in an ideal — to understand life. But life is not understood here on earth. Supersensible knowledge alone can enable us to understand it, rather than external science. It would be the wildest fantasy to believe that we could ever penetrate the laws of living things as one can physical or chemical laws. To do so remains an unattainable ideal. It is impossible to gain knowledge of life from the physical plane alone, for such understanding is the preserve of supersensible perception.

But just as sense-based knowledge of living things is impossible, so also is a *supersensible* knowledge of death. There are conditions of terrible isolation of consciousness in the worlds of spirit — there is such a thing as a temporary immersion in a sleeplike condition, but there is no death as such in the higher worlds. Death is impossible there. All the beings we have learned to know in higher hierarchies are distinguished by the fact that they do not know death, never pass through death. Just as the Bible tells us that the angels covered their faces before the secret of birth, the secret of becoming an earthly human being, so must they and all other higher beings cover their faces before death. Death is an event that is only possible in the world of the senses, not in the supersensible world.

Among all the beings of the higher worlds there

was One and One alone who had to undergo death—who, we may also say, willed to go through it. That is the Christ. It was for this that he had to descend to earth. In order for a being of the higher worlds to accomplish what was necessary for earth evolution, the Christ had to descend from a world in which there is no death to the world where death resides.

If such ideas seem abstract at first, it is up to us to transform them into feeling and experience. The full understanding of what I have now described in an abstract way will evolve as humanity does. With a certain reverence, then, with humility and delicacy, let us now approach the secret at the heart of the Mystery of Golgotha.

What was it that really took place? I have often described it. Christ descended from supersensible worlds into the world in which he has since lived as a hidden force—a force however which will reveal itself increasingly from this century onwards. He descended out of a world in which there is no death to one where there is death; and he—this force—has united himself with the earth. From being a cosmic force he has become a force of the earth. He passed through death in order to come to life in earth existence, in order to live in the earthly realm. And all through the centuries humanity has striven to understand Christ through the souls who imbued themselves with his impulse. But the nearer evolution approached to the Gabriel age, which has now passed, the more this understanding receded — until today, at the very time such understanding should exist, it is sadly lacking, and materialism prevails not only in modern science but consequently in theology too. Real understanding of the Christ impulse has diminished. Materialism has seized on human souls and rooted deeply in them. In many ways materialism became the fundamental principle underlying the epoch which has just elapsed. Countless souls died during that epoch who went through the gate of death with a materialistic outlook, something which would have been impossible in former times.

These souls then lived in the world of spirit between death and a new birth without knowing anything of the world in which they were dwelling. But then a being approached them whom they perceived in that world. They had to and could perceive him because he had united with the earth, even though he holds sway invisibly at present in physical earth existence. And the exertions of those souls who had gone through the gate of death succeeded — there is no other way to put it — in driving Christ out of the world of spirit. Christ has had to re-experience the Mystery of Golgotha, although not to the same degree. At that time he went through death. Now he had to undergo banishment from existence in the world of spirit. And thus was fulfilled in him the eternal law of the spiritual world — that what vanishes from higher spiritual existence is revealed anew in the lower world.[19]

If it is possible in the twentieth century for souls to evolve to an understanding of the Mystery of Golgotha it is because, through a kind of conspiracy of materialistic souls, Christ has been driven out of the worlds of spirit into the world of the senses, into the human world, so that in this earthly realm also a new understanding for Christ can begin to unfold. Christ has therefore become still more closely and intimately united with humanity's destiny on earth. And while in the past people could look up to Yahweh or Jehovah and know that he was the being who sent out Michael to prepare the transition from the Yahweh age to the Christ age, it is now Christ who sends Michael to us.

This is the new and important fact which we must transform into feeling experience. As formerly human beings could speak of Yahweh-Michael, the leader of the age, so now we can speak of Christ-Michael. Michael has been exalted to a higher stage — from folk spirit to epoch spirit — since becoming the messenger and Countenance of Christ. And so, when we speak of a right understanding of the Michael impulse in our age, we are speaking of a right understanding of the Christ impulse.

Abstract understanding always deals in names and designations, and thinks it gains insight simply by asking, 'What kind of being is Michael?' It desires to know which hierarchy he comes from, that he is an archangel, that archangels have such and such qualities. Then it is all wrapped up and people think they know the nature of such a being. But they do not. If one wishes to understand humanity's evolution, one has to understand that Michael too has evolved. One has to understand that the being who paved the way for the Mystery of Golgotha is the same who now, in our day, paves the way for understanding it. But then he was a folk spirit and now he is a guiding spirit of our whole times. Then he was Yahweh's messenger and now he is the messenger of Christ. We speak of Christ in the right way when we speak of Michael and his mission, knowing that Michael, who was formerly the bearer of Jehovah's mission, is now the bearer of Christ's mission ...

I have not spoken to you about the spiritual background of the world in which we live and in which we take our stand as anthroposophists in order for you to merely theorize about these things, but so that you may transform into feeling and experience what has been expressed in words and ideas. Yes, to be an anthroposophist in our age means to know the nature of the supersensible world which underlies the sense world as it has evolved, to feel oneself embedded in the world of spirit in the same way, physically, we feel ourselves in dynamic interaction with the atmosphere around us. But we do not feel ourselves to be within the world of spirit simply by repeating 'spirit, spirit, spirit is in us ...' Just as one has to measure and gauge the state of the earth's atmosphere in a real, practical way — in cloud formation, humidity and other phenomena — so we must learn to experience in a real way the spiritual world into which we plunge every night when we fall asleep. We must feel and know what lives in this world of spirit and what is now happening as a result of the mission entrusted by Christ to Michael, that is, to the same spirit of the hierarchy of archangels who in earlier times served Yahweh in preparing the Mystery of Golgotha. That is what is happening behind the evolution of our physical sense-world. And to feel ourselves permeated with such events in the world of spirit, in the same way as we feel ourselves physically permeated by the atmosphere which we breathe in and out, means to have an awareness of the world of spirit which is thoroughly real and right for our time.

Try to gather the results of esoteric enquiry I have sought to lay before you into an underlying feeling that informs your souls. Try to have a sensitive understanding of them, and be aware what it means in these particular times to live consciously in the spiritual events that are taking place around us, to live consciously in the world to which our soul goes every night when we fall asleep and from which we return every morning when we awake. Try to lead the soul into the direct, specific experience of what is so abstractly called divine providence, for our age demands this. Try now, in this present age of ours, to experience the individual beings who compose what people of past ages felt only as a vague and undefined providence at work in the world.

The task of the previous (Gabriel) epoch was to find natural science. Place this as a picture before your souls. At that time the laws of nature were useful and good in so far as they were properly used to develop external comprehension of the world in human souls. But there is nothing absolutely good or bad in this external world of maya.[20] In our own time the laws of nature would be bad if still used as the basis for human understanding of the world at a time when spiritual life is flowing into sensory experience. These words are not directed against what was accomplished in past ages, but against what tries to remain as it was in former ages, and refuses to serve the new revelation.

Michael did not fight this same dragon in past ages, for the dragon we refer to now was not yet a dragon.[21] It will become one if the concepts and ideas that belong to natural science are used to construct the world view of the coming age. The dragon is a fitting image for what wishes to rear its head in the midst of humanity, for what must be vanquished by Michael, whose age begins in our time.

That is an important imagination—Michael overcoming the dragon. To receive the influx of spiritual life into the sense-world is, from now on, a service to Michael. We serve Michael by overcoming the dragon that is trying to grow to his full strength and stature through ideas which gave rise to materialism in a previous epoch, and which now threaten to outstay their usefulness and live on into the future. To defeat this means to serve Michael. That is the victory of Michael over the dragon—an old image which for former times had another meaning but which must now acquire the right meaning for our age. When we are aware of the part we have to play as people of a new age, then our task can rise before us when we contemplate this picture of Michael conquering the dragon.

So let us take this image and inform our imagination with it. Let us try to understand our times through a precise and real awareness that we are permeated with the spiritual guidance of our age, one available to each human soul who sincerely seeks to evolve and ascend to ever higher levels of spiritual life.

TOWARDS A MICHAEL FESTIVAL

11. Thinking with Nature

Extract from a lecture given in Dornach on
1 April 1923

The core of this short passage is the need to develop a new kind of thinking that is alive not abstract, entering into rather than distancing itself from all phenomena. By truly living with the rhythm of the changing seasons we can find the power we need to create and form a Michaelmas festival that embodies and reflects authentic contemporary human experience.

Humanity must attain an esoteric maturity, developing a thinking that is not merely abstract but is so real and specific that human beings can once again create festivals. Then it will become possible once again to unite something spiritual with the earthly cycles of sense phenomena.

All our thoughts are so abstract! No matter how remarkable they are, how intelligent, life cannot penetrate them if they remain abstract. When people today reflect that Easter could be set, abstractly, on any arbitrary day, no longer accord-

ing to the constellations of the stars, when today
all higher knowledge is darkened, when the
human being no longer sees any relation between
insight into the soul and spirit, and into natural,
physical forces, it is time once again to unite
something spiritual directly with the earth's sense
phenomena...

Today people continue to celebrate festivals
according to traditional custom. But they need once
more to tap the esoteric force in themselves that
enables them to 'speak' into nature something that
accords with natural cycles. It must become possible to grasp the Michael thought as the blossom of
the Easter thought. While the Easter thought stems
from physical blossoming, it will become possible
to place the blossom of the Easter thought—the
Michael thought—into the course of the year as the
outcome of physical withering.

People must learn once more to 'think' the
spiritual along with the cycles of nature. We do
not need to indulge in esoteric speculation, but to
act esoterically. But people will only be able to do
this when they can conceive their thoughts so
specifically, in such a living way, that they do not
distance themselves from everything that is going
on around them when they think, but instead
think *with* the course of events—think along with
the fading of the leaves, the ripening of the fruits,

in a Michaelic way, just as at Easter one knows how to think with the sprouting, springing, blossoming plants and flowers.

When people understand how to think with the course of the year, then forces will intermingle with their thoughts that once again enable human beings to enter into dialogue with the divine, spiritual powers that reveal themselves from the stars. From the stars human beings first drew the power to establish festivals which have an inner human validity. Festivals must be founded out of inner, esoteric force. Then, from the dialogue with the fading, ripening plants, with the dying earth, by finding the right, inner festival mood, human beings will also once more be able to hold converse with the gods and link human and divine existence.

12. Breathing with the Year

Extract from a lecture given in Dornach on
2 April 1923

*In this passage Steiner relates the two festivals at the
equinoxes to each other, describing how Michaelmas
complements Easter. He highlights three different phases
in our human experience of the year's cycle: inbreath
(winter), outbreath (summer), and between these two a
stage of rhythmic transition where our winter separation
passes into unity with physical life at Easter, and passes
back towards separation from it at Michaelmas. This
threefold quality gained from perceiving the cycle of the
year is one, Steiner says, which can have far-reaching
effects on our understanding of social processes; and
again he highlights the importance which an authentic
Michaelmas festival could have for the social issues of our
time. Though Steiner does not explicitly say this here, the
threefold rhythm he mentions can also be seen in relation
to the human head (winter) and limbs (summer) with the
heart (equinoxes) mediating between them. In subsequent
lectures in this volume Steiner particularly emphasizes
the heart qualities of mindful feeling and courage in
relation to the Michaelmas festival.*

If the Easter thought 'He has been laid in the grave and is arisen' were to be coloured by adding to it the human thought 'He is arisen and may be laid in the grave without perishing', if this Michael thought could come to life, what tremendous significance this would have for our whole sense of things, our feeling and will, and how deeply this experience would enter into the fabric of human society.

My dear friends, all that people are hoping for from a renewal of society will not arise from all the debate and all the social forms built on external, physical perceptions. It will only come about when a mighty inspiration passes through humanity, takes hold of it, allowing the moral and spiritual dimensions of life to be felt alongside the natural and sense-perceptible dimensions.

People today are like earthworms, you can say, looking for sunlight under the ground, whereas to find it they need to surface. Nothing will in fact be accomplished by all today's organizations and plans for reform. Something can be achieved only by the mighty impact of an impulse drawn from the spirit. For it must be clear to us that the Easter thought itself can only attain its new 'nuance' when complemented by the Michael thought ...

The sprouting plant in the spring contains the spiritual within its sprouting and growing; the spiritual is mingled with the sensible in what is essentially a unity. The withering plant lets the leaf fall, and the spirit rises. We then have the spirit, the invisible, supersensible spirit, and the material that falls away from it. You can say that it is like a uniform fluid in a container in which a substance is dissolved initially; and then, by some process, we cause this to separate from the fluid and fall to the bottom as sediment. Now the two which were united are distinct.

The spring tends to weave everything together, to blend everything into a vague, undifferentiated unity. The view of the autumn, if we only look at it in the right way, if we contrast it in the right way with our view of the spring, calls attention to the way the spiritual works on the one hand and the physical and material works on the other. The Easter thought loses nothing of value if the Michaelmas thought is added to it. On the one hand we have the Easter thought where everything appears as a pantheistic mixture, you can say, a unity. Then we have the separating out and differentiation — but this does not occur in some haphazard fashion.

Think of this cyclical process: joining together, mingling, unifying; then an intermediate state as differentiation takes place; then complete separation and differentiation; then again the merging of what was differentiated, and so forth. Besides the two evident conditions there is always a third that becomes apparent in the rhythm between the differentiated and undifferentiated conditions, or you can say the intermediate state between the earth's inbreath and outbreath. Here you see a rhythm at work, a physical and spiritual dynamic of mutual interaction, in fact a mediating element of soul.

But the important thing is this: not to stop with the common human fancy that everything must be led back into a unity. Whether such unity is spiritual or material in nature this just leads us back to an undefined universal darkness. At night all cows are grey. Likewise, in spiritual monism[22] all ideas are grey, as they are too in material monism. What is important is that we as human beings can unite ourselves with the cosmic course of things in such a way as to follow the living transition from unity into trinity, then return from the trinity into unity. When by complementing the Easter thought with the Michael thought in this way we develop the capacity to perceive the primordial trinity in all existence, then we shall take this into our whole attitude of soul. Then we will be able to comprehend that in fact all life depends on the activity and interaction of primordial trinities. And when we have the Michael festival inspiring such a view in the same way that the one-sided Easter festival inspired the view now existing,[23] then we shall

have a source of inspiration, an impulse of inter-
acting nature and spirit, which gives rise to a perception of threefoldness in our observation and
active participation in life. And whether the
destructive forces of decline at work in human
evolution can be transformed into ascending forces
depends on the development of this impulse.

You can say that when we tried to introduce a
threefold impulse[24] this was in a certain sense a test
of whether the Michael thought has gained enough
strength yet, so that one senses this impulse flowing
directly out of the forces that shape our time. It was
a test of the human soul, of whether the Michael
thought is strong enough yet in a large number of
people. Well, this test produced a negative reply.
The Michael thought is not yet strong enough in a
large number of people for it to be truly perceived
in all its epoch-shaping power. It will, indeed, be
scarcely possible to unite human souls with the
necessary vital, shaping cosmic forces unless the
inspiring power that can imbue a Michael festival —
a new, creative impulse — can emerge from the
depths of esoteric life and endeavour ...

Any reference to this sort of thing today is
regarded as some kind of superstition. It is considered great wisdom to add one thing to another
and so on ad infinitum. But nature does not in fact
do this. If we look only at the realm in which

everything is interwoven in a unity, as is nature in springtime—which of course we must look at if we want to observe this interwoven whole—then we can never restore the pulse and rhythm of three.

But when anyone attends to the whole course of the year, when he sees how the 'three' is organized, how the spiritual and physical-material life are present as a duality, and the rhythmic interweaving of the two gives rise to a third element, then he perceives this three-in-one, one-in-three, and learns to know how the human being can place himself into the whole activity of the cosmos.

The human soul would become intrinsically able to penetrate and unite with the cosmos if the Michael thought could truly awaken as a festival thought—in such a way that we placed a Michael festival in the second half of September to complement the Easter festival; if to the thought of the resurrection of the god after death could be added the thought, derived from the Michael impulse, of human resurrection from death; if through Christ's resurrection the human being would find the strength to die in Christ. This means taking the risen Christ into one's soul during earthly life so as to be able to die in him, that is, to be able to 'die' not at death but during life.[25]

An inner consciousness such as this would proceed from the inspiring element that derives from a true Michael festival and service. It is easy to see how far removed from any such idea is our materialistic age, which has also grown narrow-minded and pedantic. Of course, nothing much can be expected as long as our age remains dead and abstract in its outlook. But if the same enthusiasm can be engendered with which festivals were once created and established in the world, the power with which people once shaped festivals, then this will work inspiringly, will act as a source of inspiration for our whole spiritual, cultural and social life. Then the forces we need will be present in life: not abstract spirit on the one hand and spirit-void nature on the other, but nature permeated with spirit, and spirit forming and shaping in the natural world. For these are one, and they will once again weave religion, science and art into one whole, when people understand how to conceive of the trinity. These three areas of religion, science and art will then be united in the right way in the Easter thought ... and then, at Michaelmas, will be perceived as three separate 'sisters' with one Easter mother, standing side by side and mutually complementing each other. Then the Michael thought, which could become a living festival in the year's course, would be able to work inspiringly on all domains of human life.

13. A Festival of Inner Courage

Extract from a lecture given in Dornach on
8 April 1923

*The reference below to sitting down passively and
watching the world like a 'movie' is far more relevant now
even than in Steiner's day. The TV and computer screen
dominate our lives, and it is all too easy to become the
passive recipient of 'information', rather than 'speaking'
something into the world. A festival of courage, says
Steiner, would call on our own conscious, soulful
activity.*

There will have to be a festival in honour of human
courage, of the human manifestation of the courage
of Michael. For what is it that today holds human
beings back from spirit knowledge? It is lack of soul
courage, not to say cowardice. People want to
receive everything passively, sit down in front of
the world as if it were a movie, want to allow the
microscope and telescope to tell them everything.
They do want to temper and focus the instrument of
their own spirit, of their own soul, through activity.

They do not wish to be followers of Michael, for this requires inner courage. This inner courage must be celebrated at a Michaelmas festival. Then such a festival of courage, of the inwardly courageous human soul, will radiate the quality that also imbues the other festivals of the year with their right content ...

If the festivals were formerly festivals of giving by the divine to the earthly, at which human beings received the gifts of heavenly powers directly, today, when the human being contains his capacities within himself, festivals must transform into celebrations of inward remembrance in which we inscribe into our soul what we need to perfect in ourselves.

And the most powerful festival of such remembrance will be this festival at the start of autumn, the Michaelmas festival, when all nature is speaking to us in a meaningful cosmic language. The trees are growing bare, the leaves are fading and withering. The butterflies which all summer long fluttered through the air, or bees which filled the air with their hum, begin to withdraw. Animals begin to hibernate. Everything is paralysed. Nature, whose own activity helped sustain us through spring and summer, now withdraws from us and we are thrown back upon ourselves. What must now awaken when nature forsakes us is courage of soul, and the Michael festival can be one of soul courage, soul strength and soul activity.

This is what will gradually give to this festival the character of inner remembrance. There is a monumental saying which tells us that what were once festivals of gifts to human beings will or should become, for all future times, festivals of remembrance. These monumental words which must be the linchpin of all festivals, including ones still to be created in future, are: 'This do in remembrance of me.' Here the very idea of festivals incorporates the aspect of conscious memory.

14. Creating a Michael Festival

Extract from a lecture given in Berlin on
23 May 1923

Connecting the earth with the heavens through a Michael
festival would be an active — and vital — deed involving
our full awareness and engagement.

It is possible to experience this autumn season just
as intensely as we experience spring. Just as we can
experience the death and resurrection of God at
Easter, so we can experience, in the autumn, the
resurrection of the human soul during our life on
earth, which enables us to go through death in the
right way. We must also understand what it means
for us and for our age that the soul of the earth is
exhaled at midsummer into the far reaches of the
cosmos, is there united with the stars and then
returns. He who fathoms the secrets of the earth's
journey through the course of the year will know
that the Michael force now descends with the
returning nature forces, which it did not do in former centuries. As autumn approaches and leaves

begin to fall to earth, we can therefore now go forward to meet the descent of Michael's power from the clouds.

Yes, there is a 'Michael' day in our calendars, and Michaelmas is a country festival.[26] Yet we shall not experience the present spiritually in such a way as to link human events on earth with nature's events until we once again understand the year's course and establish seasonal festivals with the inner significance that ancient peoples established through their dreamlike clairvoyant perception. In ancient times people understood the significance of the year's seasons. Through insight into mysteries such as I could only refer to in passing today, the festivals of Christmas, Easter and Midsummer were established. Nowadays we give each other presents at Christmas and do certain other things as well. But in lectures I have given on Christmas and Easter, I have often spoken of how very little people today still gain from these festivals, how everything has now assumed an external form based on mere tradition. But when the festivals which we celebrate without understanding are again understood, our spiritual understanding of the year's course will give us the strength to establish a festival which has real significance only for our present age; this will be the Michael festival. It will be a festival in the last days of September, when autumn approaches, the leaves wither, the trees grow bare and nature faces death, just as it arises in new, budding life at Easter time. At this time we can experience through the dying back of nature how the soul of the earth descends and unites with it, bringing Michael out of the clouds.

When we acquire the strength to establish such a festival out of the spirit — a festival that brings with it once more a feeling of fellowship into our social life — then we shall have founded something in our midst that has the spirit at its source. More important than all other reflections on social conditions, which can only bear fruit in our contemporary chaos if they take full account of the spirit, would be this: that a number of people with understanding for these things come together to institute on earth, in harmony with the cosmos, a Michael festival. This autumn festival would be a worthy counterpart to the Easter festival. If people could take the initiative and found a festival whose source arises only in the world of spirit, but which can kindle feelings of fellowship among human beings — a festival whose immediacy and reality would be created through the fresh, full power of the human heart — then something would come into being which can unite people once more in the social realm. In the past, festivals used to bind human beings strongly together. Just think, for instance, of all that has been done and said and thought in connection with festivals throughout civilization. All of this entered physical life through festivals established directly out of the spirit.

If people could take the initiative to establish a Michael festival worthy of the name, during the last days of September, this would be a most significant deed. But they would have to find the courage within themselves not merely to *discuss* things such as external reforms but to *do* something that connects the earth with the heavens, that reconnects physical with spiritual conditions. If the spirit was led down once more into earthly conditions this would give humanity a mighty impetus and impulse for the continuation of all life and civilization.

There is naturally no time here to describe to you the scientific, religious and artistic experiences which could arise, just as in ancient festivals, if a new festival of Michaelmas were established in a great and worthy way out of the spirit. How much more important this would be than all today's social movements and theories. What would it really mean? Does it not mean a great deal for insight into the inner nature of the human being if we can fathom another person's way of thinking or truly understand his words? And if today we can fathom the whole influence of the universe on us as autumn approaches, if we can read and decipher all the signs of its countenance, if we can draw upon its forces and work creatively with them, then the establishment of such a festival would reveal not only the will of human beings but also the will of the world of spirit. Then the spirit would dwell once more among mankind!

15. Breaking the Spell, Kindling the Fire

Lecture given in Vienna on 28 September 1923

The final lecture — given in its entirety — seems a fitting culmination to this volume, concluding with a powerful and, one could say, passionate plea for us to develop and deepen heart forces, to overcome the cowardice and disengagement pervading contemporary life, and to transform ourselves inwardly. If conviction of the reality of the spirit can come to be experienced as fully as the ground under our feet, we can release ourselves from an isolated, hermit-like existence in relation to other beings, and help benevolent forces flow into society and the natural world. The match to kindle warmth of soul is one we must strike ourselves. A Michael festival could form the lantern to bear this light into the gathering darkness — both of winter and of an era of cold intellect and conflict.

My dear friends, you will have sensed in what I was able to tell you at the close of yesterday's lecture about old traditions relating to Michael's conflict with the dragon that in our own times we need to revitalize the elements of a world view once embodied in this image. Not so long ago — even in eighteenth-century souls — this world view still lived as reality. But before I can tell you, as I will in succeeding lectures, what a genuine, contemporary spiritual perspective can and must do to revive it, I need to introduce to you, as it were in stages, a more general, anthroposophical train of thought. This will show the way in which the world view we are discussing can once again become a living force in humanity's thinking, feeling and actions.

If we observe our present relation to nature and to the whole world, and if, with sufficient openness of mind, we compare this with that of former times, we will discover that the human being has, fundamentally, become a veritable hermit in his attitude towards the cosmos and the forces at work in it. He is a hermit in so far as he enters physical life at birth and loses his memory of life before birth — a memory that was once common to all humanity. That period of our life during which, nowadays, we merely grow to full use of our capacities of mind and memory, a period which we can remember back to during our lifetime was, once upon a time, in former epochs of human evolution when real memory lit up in us, an actual retrospect of prenatal experiences as spiritual beings which we passed through prior to each life on earth. The loss of such memory is one factor that makes contemporary human beings into hermits within the cosmos; they are unaware of the connection between their earthly and spiritual states of existence.

The other factor is this: when people now gaze into the vast cosmos they observe the outer forms of the stars and constellations, but no longer have any inner relationship to what is spiritual in the cosmos. In fact, people of today observe the kingdoms of nature that surround them on earth — the manifold beauty of plants, the mighty shapes of mountains, the fleeting forms of clouds and so on. Yet here again they are restricted to their sense impressions and are often even alarmed if they feel a deeper, more intimate contact with the great spaces of nature, fearing they might lose their analytic attitude towards them. This phase of human evolution has been vital in the development of what we experience in an awareness of freedom, the feeling of freedom — in order to achieve full self-awareness, the inner strength that permits the full unfolding of the ego. But necessary as this hermit life of humanity was in relation to the universe, it must be no more than a transition to another epoch in which the human being finds his way back to the spirit, which after all underlies all things and beings. And it is this very endeavour to find our way back to the spirit which we must engage in by grasping the

Michael idea in its right sense and true form, the form it has to assume in our time.

Our thinking, our heart and mind,[27] and our life of action all need to be permeated with the Michael impulse. But when it is stated that a Michael festival should be reinstated, and that the time is ripe for assigning it a place alongside the other festivals of the year, it is of course not enough for a few people to say, 'Well, let's start, let's have a Michael festival then!' My dear friends, if anthroposophy is to achieve its aim, the superficiality so prevalent today must obviously play no part. Instead, whatever may grow out of anthroposophy must do so in profound earnestness. And in order to understand what this earnestness means, we need to reflect on how festivals — once vital, and today so anaemic — took their place in human evolution. Did the Christmas or Easter festival arise because a few people formed the idea of establishing a festival at a certain time of year, and decided to organize it? Of course not. For something like the Christmas festival to enter humanity, Jesus Christ had to be born. This event had to take place and enter the earth's history and evolution — a transcendent event. And the Easter festival? It could never have had any real meaning if it had not commemorated what took place at the Mystery of Golgotha, had this event not been an incisive intervention for humanity's evolution. If these festivals have faded nowadays in significance, if the whole earnestness of the Christmas and Easter festivals is no longer felt, this fact itself should lead to their intensification through a more profound understanding of the birth of Christ and the Mystery of Golgotha. But under no circumstances should we imagine adding to these festivals simply by superficially establishing a Michael festival at the beginning of autumn. Something must be present that is incisive for human evolution in the same way — though possibly to a lesser degree — as were all events that led to festivals being established.

The possibility of celebrating a Michael festival must be developed, based on insight arising from the anthroposophical movement. But just as the Christmas and Easter festivals resulted from actual, objective events in humanity's evolution, so a radical transformation must take place in humanity's inner essence before such a step is taken. Anthroposophy must become a profound experience, an experience people can regard in a way similar to what they feel when imbued with the whole power dwelling in the birth of Jesus Christ or in the Mystery of Golgotha. As was said, this may be true to a lesser degree in the case of the Michael festival, yet something of this soul-transmuting power must proceed from the anthroposophical movement. That, indeed, is what we long for: an imbuing of anthroposophy with this power to transform souls. And this can only occur if the substance of its teaching—if I may call it that—becomes actual, lived experience.

Let us now turn our attention to the kinds of experiences that can enter our inner experience through anthroposophy. As you know, we distinguish the soul forces of thinking, feeling and will. And in connection with feeling, particularly, we speak of the human heart.[28] Our thinking appears cold and dry to us—colourless—and as though spiritually anaemic when our thoughts assume an abstract form, when we are unable to imbue them with the warmth and enthusiasm of feeling. We can call someone a full and feeling person only when something of his heart and mind's inner warmth streams forth to us when he utters his thoughts. And we can really only establish close contact with a person if his conduct towards us and the world is not merely correct and dictated by duty, but if his actions show enthusiasm, a warm heart, a love of nature and love for every being. This human heart and mind, then, dwells you can say at the very core of soul life.

But while thinking and will have assumed a certain character due to the human being's retreat into a hermit-like state in relation to the cosmos, this is even truer of his disposition of heart. Thinking may contemplate the perfection of its calculations, and perhaps rejoice at their subtlety, but it simply fails to sense how fundamentally remote it is from the warm heartbeat of life. And right actions carried out merely through a sense of duty, without being sustained by real feeling, may give people a sense of satisfaction, but such dutiful conduct is in fact only half a life. Neither the one nor the other touch the human soul very intimately. But what lies between thinking and will, everything comprised in the feeling mind and thinking heart[29] is intimately connected with our whole being. And while it may seem, due to the particular tendencies at work in modern human beings, as though elements that should warm and elevate the human heart and mind can become chilly as well, this is an illusion. While our conscious inner experiences may lack a heartfelt quality, this lack will inevitably harm us as full human beings. And if we endure this—if we compel ourselves to lack a soulful, heartfelt engagement and awareness—this will in some way or other gnaw at our whole being, will eat right down into our physical organization and affect our health. Much of what appears today as symptoms of decline is fundamentally connected with the lack of heartfelt awareness into which many people have subsided. The full significance of these rather general statements will become clearer as we delve further.

Someone who grows up in and enters into contemporary civilization observes the things of the outer world. He perceives them, forms abstract thoughts about them, possibly derives genuine pleasure from a lovely blossom or a majestic plant. And if he is at all imaginative he may even form a living inner picture of it. Yet he remains completely unaware of his relation to that world of which the plant, for example, forms a part. Just to speak of spirit, spirit and again spirit is far from enough to develop spiritual perception. What we need, instead, is to become aware of our real spiritual relationship to the things around us. When we observe a plant in the usual way we do not in the least sense the presence of an elemental being dwelling in it, of something spiritual. We do not dream that every plant harbours something which is not satisfied by us examining it and forming the kind of abstract mental images we are used to. For in every plant is concealed — as though enchanted — an elemental spiritual being. And only they properly observe a plant who realize that this outer loveliness is the sheath concealing an enchanted spiritual being — a relatively insignificant being, to be sure, in the great scale of cosmic interrelationships, but nevertheless a being intimately related to the human being.

We are really so closely linked to the world that we cannot take a step into nature without falling under the direct influence exercised on us by our intimate relationship with everything. And when we see a lily growing from seed to blossom we must vividly imagine — though not personified — that this lily awaits and requires something from us. While unfolding its leaves, and especially its blossom, this lily really expects something. The spirit of the lily (I have to use human language although it is not quite adequate to express inherent realities) says to itself as it were: 'People will pass by and look at me; and when a sufficient number of human eyes have directed their gaze at me, the spell of my enchantment will be broken, and I will be able to start on my journey into worlds of spirit.' You may naturally object that many lilies grow unseen by human eyes. Yes, but then the conditions are different, and such lilies find their release in a different way. The law that decrees that a particular lily's spell will be broken by human eyes arises at the first human glance upon it. It is a relationship between man and lily which both enter into. These elemental beings are all around us, begging us not to look at flowers so abstractly nor form such abstract images of them, but rather to let our heart and mind enter into what lives as soul and spirit in the flowers, imploring us to break their spell of enchantment. Human life should really be engaged in continuously releasing from enchantment the elemental spirits imprisoned in minerals, plants and animals.[30]

An idea such as this can readily be sensed in its abundant beauty. But when we grasp it in its full spiritual significance we can also feel the responsibility we thereby incur towards the whole cosmos. At the present epoch of civilization—when we are developing human freedom—our attitude towards the flowers is mere sipping at what we should really be drinking. We sip by forming concepts and ideas whereas we should really drink deeply by uniting, through our heartfelt awareness, with the elemental spirits of the things and beings that surround us.

As I said, we do not need to consider the lilies never seen by human eyes, but must concern ourselves with those that are seen, because they require a relationship with our heartfelt human awareness. An effect proceeds from the lily; and diverse, mighty and magnificent indeed are the spiritual effects that continually approach us from natural things when we walk amongst them. Those who have insight into such things continually perceive the diversity and grandeur of all that streams out to them from nature's elemental spirituality. It flows out and into them, streaming continually towards them as a supersensible spirituality poured out over external nature, which is a mirror of divine spiritual realms.

In the following days we will come to speak more of these matters in detail. At present I just wish to say that in the human being there dwells the force I have described as the force of the dragon whom Michael encounters, and against whom he does battle. I said that this dragon is animal-like in form, yet is really a supersensible being; that on account of his arrogant refusal to submit to higher laws he was expelled into the sense world where he now has his existence. And I said further that he exists only within the human being, because nature cannot harbour him. External nature, the image of divine spirituality, has an innocence completely unrelated to the dragon. The latter is established in the human being, as I have stated.[31] But as a supersensible being in the sense world he instantly attracts the supersensible elemental forces that stream towards human beings out of nature, and unites with them — with the result that, instead of releasing plant elementals from their spell of enchantment through the power of our heart and soul, we unite them with the dragon, allowing them to perish with the dragon in our lower nature. For everything in the world moves in an evolutionary stream, taking many different directions to this end. And the elemental beings dwelling in minerals, plants and animals must rise to a higher existence than is offered by their present abodes. They can only accomplish this *by passing through the human being.* Establishing a worldly civilization is not our sole purpose on earth. We also have a cosmic purpose within the overall sweep of universal evolution, and this cosmic purpose is linked with what I have just described — with the further development of those elemental beings that are at a low stage in earth existence, but are destined for a higher one. When we human beings enter into a certain relationship with them, and when everything proceeds as it should, they can attain to this higher stage of evolution.

In ancient times of instinctive human evolution, when the forces of soul and spirit shone forth from human hearts and minds, and when these forces were as much a matter of course as were the forces of nature, world evolution occurred, you can say, in a normal, orderly way as the flux of existence streamed through human beings. But during the age that must now meet its end, that must instead advance to a higher form of spirituality, untold elemental substance within the human being has been delivered over to the dragon — whose very nature it is to hunger and thirst for these elemental beings, to creep about dismaying plants and minerals, gorging himself on nature's elemental beings. He wishes to unite with them, and to permeate his own being with them. He cannot do this in the natural world external to human beings, but only within them, for that is the only place he can dwell. And if this process were to continue the earth would be doomed, for the dragon would inevitably be victorious in earthly existence.

He would be victorious for a very definite reason. By virtue of saturating himself, as it were, with elemental beings in human nature, something occurs in body, soul and spirit. As far as the mind and spirit are concerned, no human being would ever arrive at the ridiculous belief in a purely material external world as assumed by contemporary science. He would never come to accept dead atoms and the like, nor assume the existence of such laws as the conservation of force and energy, or of the permanence of matter, if the dragon were not within him to absorb the elemental beings approaching him from without. When these enter into the human being, enter the body of the dragon within us, human observation is distracted from the spiritual content of things. We no longer see spirit in what has entered us, but only dead matter. In terms of soul, everything anyone has ever expressed as what I must call cowardice results from the dragon having absorbed the elemental powers within him. O, how widespread is this cowardice of soul! We know very well what we should do, that such and such a thing is the right course of action in a given situation, but we cannot bring ourselves to do it; a certain dead weight acts in our soul — the elemental beings in the dragon's body are at work in us. And lastly, in terms of the body, we would never be plagued by what are called 'germs' of disease if our body had not been prepared — through the spiritual results of what I have just described — as a soil for these germs. These things penetrate right into our physical organization. It is true to say that a proper perception of the human spirit, soul and body today finds that we are cut off from the realm of spirit in three directions. But this is for a good purpose: the attainment of freedom. We no longer have in us the spiritual powers we might have. And thus you see that this threefold debilitation of human life, this glutted dragon within us, prevents us from experiencing the potency of the spirit within us.

There are two ways of experiencing anthroposophy — with a wide range of variations between these two ends of the spectrum. The first is this. Someone sits down in a chair, picks up a book, and finds it quite interesting and comforting to learn that there is such a thing as spirit, as immortality. It just suits him to know that the soul does not die when the body does. He derives greater satisfaction from such an outlook than from a materialistic one. He adopts it as one might adopt an abstract reflection on geography, except that anthroposophy provides more comfort than that. Yes, that is one way. The person gets up from his chair really no different from what he was when he sat down, except for having derived a certain satisfaction from what he read — or heard if it was a lecture rather than a book.

But there is also another way of receiving what anthroposophy has to offer. It is to absorb something like the idea of Michael's conflict with the dragon so that you are inwardly transformed; to feel it as an important, incisive experience, and to rise from your chair a fundamentally different person after reading something like this. As I said, there are all sorts of shades in the spectrum between these two extremes.

The first type of reader cannot be counted on at all when it is a question of reviving and revitalizing the Michaelmas festival. Only those can be depended upon who are determined, as far as their capacities allow, to take up anthroposophy as something living and transformative. And precisely this is what people should experience within the anthroposophical movement: the need to experience the life-forces in ideas that first present themselves to us merely as that, as ideas. But now I wish to say something completely paradoxical. It is sometimes much easier to understand the opponents of anthroposophy than its adherents. The opponents say: 'Oh, these anthroposophical ideas are fantasy, they conform with no reality.' And they reject them, remain untouched by them. One can readily understand this kind of attitude, and find a variety of reasons for it. As a rule it is caused by real though unconscious fear of these ideas. But it also often happens that someone accepts these ideas, yet, despite diverging so radically from everything else in the world that can be accepted, they produce less feeling in him than would an electric current applied to his knuckle. In the latter case he at least feels a twitching produced by the spark; and the absence of a similar spark in the soul is often the cause of great anguish. This is related to the need of our time for human beings to receive the imprint of the spirit, to be grasped by it, and not just by all that is physical reality. People avoid being knocked about and shaken physically, but they do not avoid coming into contact with ideas relating to other worlds, ideas that arise as something very distinct in today's sense-bound world, but then maintaining the same indifference towards them as towards ideas produced by the senses.

The capacity to elevate oneself to the point at which thoughts of the spirit can grip us as powerfully as can anything in the physical world is Michaelic power. It is confidence in the ideas of spirit which, given the capacity to receive them at all, lead to the certainty that can be expressed as follows: 'I have received a spiritual impulse, I give myself up to it, I become the instrument of its realization.' First failure—never mind! Second failure—never mind! A hundred failures are of no consequence, for no failure is ever a decisive factor in judging the truth of a spiritual impulse whose effect has been inwardly grasped. We have full confidence in a spiritual impulse, grasped at a certain point of time, only when we can say to ourselves: 'My hundred failures prove, at most, that the conditions for realizing this impulse are not given me in this incarnation.[32] But the nature of this impulse tells me that it is right. And if I have to wait a hundred incarnations for the power to realize this impulse, nothing but its own nature can convince me of the efficacy or impotence of any spiritual impulse.'

If you will imagine this thought developed in the human heart and mind as great confidence in the spirit, if you will consider that the human being can cling to something he has seen to be spiritually victorious, as firmly as to a rock, and refuse to relinquish it despite all external opposition, then you will have an idea of what the Michael power, the Michael being really demands of us; for only then will you grasp the nature of spiritual conviction. We may leave some spiritual impulse in abeyance, even for a whole lifetime. But once we have grasped it we must never waver in cherishing it within us, for only then can we store it up for subsequent incarnations. And when confidence in the spirit has thus established a frame of mind to which spiritual reality appears as real as the ground under our feet that upholds us, then we shall have in our hearts and minds a feeling of what Michael really expects of us.

Undoubtedly you will admit that in the course of recent centuries—even the last thousand years of human history—this active confidence in the spirit has been waning on a huge scale, and that life does not help most human beings develop such confidence. Yet this had to happen. Human beings have burned the bridges that formerly connected them with the power of Michael.

In a certain sense we have deserted and turned our backs on the Michael power. The stark materialism of the nineteenth century is a revolt against the Michael power. But objectively, in the domain of macrocosmic spirit, the Michael power has been victorious, precisely in the last third of the nineteenth century. What the dragon hoped to achieve through human evolution will not come to pass. Yet at the same time what we are now conjuring up is the fact that the free resolve of human beings will be required to take part in Michael's victory over the dragon. And this involves finding ways to abandon the human passivity that still prevails in relation to spirit, and enter into an active relationship with it. Michael forces cannot be acquired through any form of passivity, not even through imploring prayer, but only by making ourselves the instruments of divine, spiritual forces by means of our loving will. The Michael forces do not wish to be implored. They desire human beings to unite with them—something they can do by bringing inner activity and energy to bear on the teachings of the world of spirit.

This tells us what needs to arise in human beings if the Michael thought is to revive. We must really become able to experience the spirit, and acquire this experience entirely through thinking, rather than some sort of clairvoyance. We would be in a bad way if everybody had to become clairvoyant in order to have this confidence in spirit. Everyone who is at all receptive to the teachings of spiritual science can have this confidence. When people imbue themselves with ever-increasing confidence in the spirit, something like an inspiration will dawn in them. And this is something for which all the good spirits of the world are waiting. Then people will experience the spring, sensing the beauty and loveliness of the plant world and finding deep delight in its sprouting, burgeoning life. But at the same time they will acquire a heartfelt sense in their souls telling them that every blossom bears testimony to the existence of an enchanted elemental being needing to be released by them. And they will learn to feel such an elemental being's longing to be released by them, instead of being delivered up to the dragon to whom it is related through its own invisibility. And then, when flowers wither in autumn, people will know that they have succeeded in contributing a little to the progress of the spirit in the world, by enabling an elemental being to slip from its plant when the blossoms wither and fall and become seed. But they will only be able to do so to the extent that they have permeated themselves with the powerful strength of Michael, thus leading this elemental being up to the spirit for which it yearns.

And people will once again experience the cycle of the seasons: spring as the birth of elemental beings longing for the spirit, and autumn as their liberation from the dying plants and withering blossoms. They will no longer stand alone as cosmic hermits who have merely grown half a year older by autumn than they were in spring. In companionship with evolving nature they will have advanced a small distance. They will not merely have inhaled physical oxygen so and so many times, but will have participated in nature's evolution, in the enchantment and disenchantment of spiritual beings in nature. People will no longer only feel themselves growing older, but will sense the transformation of nature as part of their destiny; they will coalesce with all that grows there, will expand in their being because their free individuality can pour itself out in sacrifice into the cosmos. This is what human beings will be able to contribute to Michael's victorious battle with the dragon.

So we can see that a Michaelmas festival is only possible when it becomes an event of the human mind, heart and soul, one that can once again experience the cycle of the seasons as a living reality. Do not imagine you are experiencing this simply by establishing an abstract concept in your mind! This can be achieved only by absorbing anthroposophy so that you look with new eyes at every plant and stone; and only when anthroposophy has taught you a new way of contemplating human life.

I have tried to give you a kind of picture of what must develop within the human heart and mind if people are to feel nature as intrinsically part of them. The most that people have retained of this sort of experience is the capacity to experience a certain soul element in their blood circulation, alongside the material aspect. Unless they are out-and-out materialists they have retained a sense of that. But to experience the pulse of external nature as we do our innermost being, to participate in the cycle of the seasons as we participate in the life within our own skin, is the preparation needed to found a Michael festival.

In so far as these lectures aim to accentuate the relationship between anthroposophy and the human heart and soul, it is my wish that they will really be gasped not merely by the head but especially by the forces of heartfelt awareness.[33] All anthroposophy is largely futile if not absorbed by this heartfelt awareness, if it carries no warmth into this mindfulness of heart. Recent centuries have piled up great stores of cleverness and ingenuity. As far as thinking is concerned, people are no longer even aware of how clever they are. True, many people regard contemporary humanity as stupid; but granted that stupid people do exist, this is really only because their cleverness has assumed such proportions that the debility of their heart and soul prevents them from knowing what to do with all their cleverness. Whenever someone is called stupid I always maintain that this is because he does not know what use to make of his cleverness. I have listened to many discussions in which some speaker or other was ridiculed as stupid — but occasionally one or other of these seemed to me to be the cleverest.

The last few centuries have developed abundant cleverness in us. But what we need today is warmth of heart and soul, and this is what anthroposophy can provide. When someone studying anthroposophy says it leaves him cold, he reminds me of someone who keeps piling wood in a stove and then complains that the room doesn't get warm. All he needs to do is kindle the wood, then it will get warm. Anthroposophy is the soul's good wood and fuel, but each must kindle it for and within himself. What everyone must find in his heartfelt awareness is the match to kindle anthroposophy. Anthroposophy is truly warm and bright, the very heart of the mindful soul, and anyone who finds it cold and intellectual just lacks the means of kindling it so it pervades him with its fire. And just as only a small match is needed to light the mundane wood, so anthroposophy too needs only a little match to catch light. But when it does, this will kindle the Michael power within us.

I want to fire everyone
with the spirit of the cosmos,
so each becomes flame,
unfolds the fiery
being of his being.

Others would rather
draw water from the cosmos
to quench the flames,
to douse the inner
spark of all being.

O joy when the human flame
is incandescent even at rest!
O bitterness when, wretched, man
is bound, held back from rousing himself.

Afterword

As I was working on this volume a poem by Gerard Manley Hopkins came into my mind. The poem, written in the autumn of 1877, two years before the date which Steiner refers to as the beginning of the age of Michael, suddenly seemed to me to prefigure a new epoch in which the human being can meet the spiritual world in a much more direct and — for want of a better word — tangible way than was previously possible. The 'summer' that 'ends now' also struck me as the passing of an age when humanity was rightly sustained by the physical world.

In one of his lectures (included here, page 32), Steiner says:

> Out of spiritual cloud formations, you can say, the figure of Michael appears to us with positive, searching and directing gaze, his eyes like a guiding sign, its gaze sent outwards, never drawn back into himself . . .

Hopkins's poem begins with a powerful evocation of the clouds, from which one can sense an elemental presence emerging. In the second verse this presence takes shape as a living being, giving a profoundly real response to the seeking heart. Steiner refers to Michael as the countenance of Christ, and here the looks and lips of a divine presence utter a greeting of acknowledgement and love. The third verse develops this realization of the vast spiritual dimension behind all of nature—as though the veil of the material world had suddenly grown thin, allowing the poet to see his Saviour through it.

In the last lecture in this volume Steiner makes what feels like an impassioned plea for our participation in the natural world to release it—and us—from enchantment. In the last four lines of his poem, Hopkins likewise sings of a powerful force that is set free when, in a way very reminiscent of Steiner's emphasis on *Gemüt* or heartfelt awareness, the bold heart of the beholder penetrates to all that lies beyond merely material reality. The very language of the poem, too, like all of Hopkins's work, seems resonant with an awareness of the transforming, revitalizing power that can flood us when we reconnect to the full— and perhaps alarming—force of a spiritual dimension, for which ordinary speech is not sufficient.

Here is the poem:

Hurrahing in Harvest

Summer ends now; now barbarous in beauty, the
    stooks rise
  Around; up above, what wind-walks! what
    lovely behaviour
  Of silk-sack clouds! has wilder, wilful-wavier
Meal-drift moulded ever and melted across
    skies?

I walk, I lift up heart, eyes,
  Down all that glory in the heavens to glean our
    Saviour;
  And, éyes, heárt, what looks, what lips yet gave
    you a
Rapturous love's greeting of realer, of rounder
    replies?

And the azurous hung hills are his world-
    wielding shoulder
  Majestic—as a stallion stalwart, very violet-
    sweet!—
These things, these things were here and but the
    beholder
  Wanting; which two when they once meet,
The heart réars wings bold and bolder
  And hurls for him, O half hurls earth for him
    off under his feet.

Gerard Manley Hopkins, 1877

Notes

1. Quoted in: *Brother Eagle, Sister Sky*, Puffin Books, 1993.
2. Anthroposophy is the name Steiner gave to the body of knowledge and activity of enquiry into the human being and the cosmos which he developed. Literally it means 'wisdom of the human being'.
3. For more on elemental nature spirits, see the last lecture in this volume and also R. Steiner: *Nature Spirits*, Rudolf Steiner Press, 2001.
4. See companion volume in this series on the St John's festival.
5. Ahriman is the name Steiner gives to the entity who seeks to fetter the human being to the earth as a merely animal and material being, denying our spiritual nature.
6. Nature beings — see note 3 above.
7. At midsummer, according to Steiner, nature is more open and closer to planetary influences.
8. Steiner describes four 'sheaths' of the human being: physical, etheric, astral and I or ego. The invisible etheric or life body is the 'body of formative forces', which imbues the dead mineral nature of matter with life and is typified by the burgeoning plant kingdom. The soul or astral body, which we share with animals, is the seat of all emotions, drives and passions. We

alone amongst natural creatures also possess an ego or I, the essence of a conscious, self-reflecting human being.

9. Jacob Boehme, 1575–1624, German mystic and Hermetic cosmologist, was a central figure in the development of esoteric philosophy, idealism, Romanticism and Protestant theology.

10. See note 5 above.

11. Phantom here does not refer to anything illusory or ghostlike, but to the way a human being would appear if this sulphur aspect was the only visible process constituting him.

12. Also known as the Akashic Records, the astral light bears an imprint of all thoughts, and can be 'read' by those with a faculty of perception for it.

13. See note 5 above.

14. See also poem by Gerard Manley Hopkins in the Afterword.

15. 'Ah' is the sound given to this letter in German, rather than the English 'A'.

16. Another name for the Dark Age.

17. See R. Steiner: *The Incarnation of Ahriman*, Rudolf Steiner Press 2006.

18. Forerunner of the United Nations.

19. It is striking that Christ therefore underwent a parallel kind of expulsion to that undergone by Ahriman (see page 37), although brought about by quite opposite causes.

20. Sanskrit word for the 'world of appearance'.

21. Elsewhere Steiner refers to the dragon of ancient

times as 'Lucifer' who was cast not into hell but 'into human heads', seeking to distance human beings from full earth experience. Lucifer is the other aspect of the duality of evil, and between him and Ahriman (see note 5) Christ holds the pivotal balance.

22. 'A philosophical theory that all being may ultimately be referred to one category; thus idealism, pantheism and materialism are monisms, as opposed to the dualism of matter and spirit' (*Chambers Dictionary*).

23. Steiner is referring here to contemporary views of the primacy of physical life and growth.

24. See R. Steiner: *Towards Social Renewal*, Rudolf Steiner Press 1999.

25. Death in the sense of entering into spiritual existence.

26. In former times, and still today in some farming communities, for instance, a special loaf or cake was baked at Michaelmas consisting of all the different grains grown on the farm during the year. There are many country traditions relating to harvest and Michaelmas, the most well known of which may be the fertility symbol of braided corn dollies. Harvest festivals of course give thanks for the earth's bounty, but such services focus primarily on physical fruitfulness rather than spiritual renewal as nature dies.

27. The German word translated by 'heart and mind' is *Gemüt*, which is fairly untranslatable, but is a kind of holistic concept of 'mind and heart', or feeling intellect. There is no single term in English that wholly corresponds with this word, but 'heart' in its widest

sense including the idea of 'heart-imbued thinking' probably comes closest to it.

28. See note 27 above.

29. *Gemüt* (see note 27 above).

30. Shakespeare's *The Tempest* gives a vivid picture of the enchantment of an elemental being Ariel, though in this case his master Prospero intentionally maintains the enchantment for his own ends. Release for Ariel does eventually come at the end of the play.

31. In the previous lecture in this sequence Steiner speaks of the human being as the dragon's fortress.

32. This refers to anthroposophy's teaching of the reincarnation of the human spirit; we all undergo incarnations in different ages, thus participating in the evolution of humanity and the world.

33. *Gemüt* (see note 27 above).

Sources

Numbers relate to section numbers in this volume.

1. Vienna, 1 October 1923, in: *Michaelmas and the Soul Forces of Man*, Anthroposophic Press, New York 1982.
2. Vienna, 30 September 1923, in: *Michaelmas and the Soul Forces of Man*, Anthroposophic Press, New York 1982.
3. Dornach, 2 April 1923, in: *The Cycle of the Year*, Anthroposophic Press, 1984
4. Stuttgart, 15 October 1923, in: *The Festivals and their Meaning*, Rudolf Steiner Press, 1996.
5. Vienna, 30 September 1923, in: *Michaelmas and the Soul Forces of Man*, Anthroposophic Press, New York 1982.
6. Dornach 5 October 1923, in: *Four Seasons and the Archangels*, Rudolf Steiner Press, 1996.
7. Dornach, 13 January 1924, *The Festivals and their Meaning*, Rudolf Steiner Press, 1996.
8. Dornach, 28 July 1924, in: *Karmic Relationships, vol. 3*, Rudolf Steiner Press, 1977.
9. Dornach, 23 November 1919, in: *The Mission of the Archangel Michael*, Anthroposophic Press, 1994.
10. Stuttgart, 20 May 1913, in: *The Festivals and their Meaning*, Rudolf Steiner Press, 1996.
11. Dornach, 1 April 1923, in: *The Cycle of the Year*, Anthroposophic Press, 1984.

12. Dornach, 2 April 1923, in: *The Cycle of the Year*, Anthroposophic Press, 1984.
13. Dornach, 8 April 1923, in: *The Cycle of the Year*, Anthroposophic Press, 1984.
14. Berlin, 23 May 1923, in: *The Festivals and their Meaning*, Rudolf Steiner Press, 1996.
15. Vienna, 28 September 1923, in: *Michaelmas and the Soul Forces of Man*, Anthroposophic Press, New York 1982.

The two verses by Steiner which begin and end the volume come from two volumes in the Meditations series, *Breathing the Spirit* and *The Heart of Peace*, both published by Rudolf Steiner Press, 2002.

Further Reading

Rudolf Steiner's fundamental books:

Knowledge of the Higher Worlds
also published as: *How to Know Higher Worlds*

Occult Science
also published as: *An Outline of Esoteric Science*

Theosophy

The Philosophy of Freedom
also published as:
Intuitive Thinking as a Spiritual Path

Some relevant volumes of Rudolf Steiner's lectures:

Christmas
Easter
St John's
Whitsun

The Four Seasons and the Archangels

For all titles contact Rudolf Steiner Press (UK) or
SteinerBooks (USA):
www.rudolfsteinerpress.com www.steinerbooks.org

Note Regarding Rudolf Steiner's Lectures

The lectures and addresses contained in this volume have been translated from the German, which is based on stenographic and other recorded texts that were in most cases never seen or revised by the lecturer. Hence, due to human errors in hearing and transcription, they may contain mistakes and faulty passages. Every effort has been made to ensure that this is not the case. Some of the lectures were given to audiences more familiar with anthroposophy; these are the so-called 'private' or 'members' lectures. Other lectures, like the written works, were intended for the general public. The difference between these, as Rudolf Steiner indicates in his *Autobiography*, is twofold. On the one hand, the members' lectures take for granted a background in and commitment to anthroposophy; in the public lectures this was not the case. At the same time, the members' lectures address the concerns and dilemmas of the members, while the public work speaks directly out of Steiner's own understanding of universal needs. Nevertheless, as Rudolf Steiner stresses: 'Nothing was ever said that was not solely the result of my direct experience of the growing content of anthroposophy. There was never any question of concessions to the prejudices and preferences of the members. Whoever reads these privately printed lectures can take them to represent anthroposophy in the fullest sense. Thus it was possible without hesitation—when the complaints in this direction became too persistent—to depart from the custom of circulating this material "For members only". But it must be borne in mind that faulty passages do occur in these reports not revised by myself.' Earlier in the same chapter, he states: 'Had I been able to correct them [the private lectures], the restriction *for members only* would have been unnecessary from the beginning.'

The original German editions on which this text is based were published by Rudolf Steiner Verlag, Dornach, Switzerland in the collected edition (*Gesamtausgabe*, 'GA') of Rudolf Steiner's work. All publications are edited by the Rudolf Steiner Nachlassverwaltung (estate), which wholly owns both Rudolf Steiner Verlag and the Rudolf Steiner Archive.

Rudolf Steiner
Easter
An Introductory Reader

Chapters: Can we Celebrate Easter?; The Earth and the Cosmos; Rising Sun, Nature and Resurrection; Golgotha, the Central Deed of Evolution; Easter, a Festival for the Future.

160pp; 978 185584 139 0; £6.99

Rudolf Steiner
Christmas
An Introductory Reader

Chapters: Christmas in a Grievous Age; Christmas and
the Earth; Delving to the Core; The Child and the Tree;
Towards a New Christmas.

168pp; 978 185584 189 5; £6.99

Rudolf Steiner
St John's
An Introductory Reader

Chapters: Midsummer Dream, the Earth Breathes Out;
Finding the Greater Self; 'He Must Increase, I Must
Decrease'; Creating Vision.

112pp; 978 185584 174 1; £5.99

Rudolf Steiner
Whitsun and Ascension
An Introductory Reader

Chapters: Rising to the Clouds, Tethered to Earth;
Suffering's Open Door; All One to Alone to One in All;
Human Freedom and the Word.

128pp; 978 1 85584 169 7; £5.99